Buy—DON'T Hold

Buy—DON'T Hold

Investing with ETFs Using Relative Strength to Increase Returns with Less Risk

Leslie N. Masonson

Vice President, Publisher: Tim Moore
Associate Publisher and Director of Marketing: Amy Neidlinger
Executive Editor: Jim Boyd
Editorial Assistant: Pamela Boland
Development Editor: Russ Hall
Operations Manager: Gina Kanouse
Senior Marketing Manager: Julie Phifer
Publicity Manager: Laura Czaja
Assistant Marketing Manager: Megan Colvin
Cover Designer: Chuti Prasertsith
Managing Editor: Kristy Hart
Project Editor: Betsy Harris
Copy Editor: Cheri Clark
Proofreader: Williams Woods Publishing Services
Indexer: WordWise Publishing Services
Compositor: Nonie Ratcliff
Manufacturing Buyer: Dan Uhrig

Published by Pearson Education, Inc.
Publishing as FT Press
Upper Saddle River, New Jersey 07458

This book is sold with the understanding that neither the author nor the publisher is engaged in rendering legal, accounting, or other professional services or advice by publishing this book. Each individual situation is unique. Thus, if legal or financial advice or other expert assistance is required in a specific situation, the services of a competent professional should be sought to ensure that the situation has been evaluated carefully and appropriately. The author and the publisher disclaim any liability, loss, or risk resulting directly or indirectly, from the use or application of any of the contents of this book.

FT Press offers excellent discounts on this book when ordered in quantity for bulk purchases or special sales. For more information, please contact U.S. Corporate and Government Sales, 1-800-382-3419, corpsales@pearsontechgroup.com. For sales outside the U.S., please contact International Sales at international@pearson.com.

Company and product names mentioned herein are the trademarks or registered trademarks of their respective owners.

Printed in the United States of America

Second Printing June 2010

ISBN-10: 0-13-704532-8
ISBN-13: 978-0-13-704532-7

Pearson Education LTD.
Pearson Education Australia PTY, Limited
Pearson Education Singapore, Pte. Ltd.
Pearson Education North Asia, Ltd.
Pearson Education Canada, Ltd.
Pearson Educatión de Mexico, S.A. de C.V.
Pearson Education—Japan
Pearson Education Malaysia, Pte. Ltd.

Library of Congress Cataloging-in-Publication Data
Masonson, Leslie N.
  Buy—don't hold : investing with ETFs using relative strength to increase returns with less risk / Leslie N. Masonson.
    p. cm.
  ISBN 978-0-13-704532-7 (hardback : alk. paper) 1. Exchange traded funds. 2. Portfolio management. I. Title.
  HG6043.M37 2010
  332.63'27—dc22
                                                    2009048632

To my loving and supportive wife Marilyn.
To my wonderful children Dan and his wife Laurie,
Amy and her husband Seth,
and my precious and beautiful grandchildren—
Brooke, Andie, Matthew, and Katie—who
have enriched our lives.

And to investors looking for a better way
to invest their hard-earned money.

May you all enjoy a profitable ride
on the stock market roller coaster.

Contents

Foreword

In these tumultuous times in the global financial markets and the 24/7 flow of information and misinformation, the individual investor is not well served by following the buy-and-hold mantra promulgated by financial institutions, mutual funds, and brokerages over the past 50 years. As of November 30, 2009, the inflation-adjusted total return of the S&P 500 for the past 10 years is still negative and has been for over a year. That means that those who retired in 1999 and put their hard-earned retirement money in a market index such as the S&P 500 (because it always goes up, right?) have not earned a penny in the past ten years. If they pay an annual fee for account maintenance, do not reinvest the dividends, or have a systematic withdrawal to live on, they are truly hurting. During the past decade, younger investors have also not performed any better, and their children's 529 plans have also taken a hit, depending on when the funds were invested.

The "world of finance" and "Wall Street" have set the stage for investing for the long term in their onslaught of tactics to market themselves and sell investing ideas to an unsuspecting and financially uneducated public. A huge emphasis is put on diversification and how it will protect you for the long term. They have confused buy-and-hold with buy-and-hope. Commissions and fees are the fuel for most of their effort. I could go on and on about the misinformation that pours out of the financial institutions.

Corporate pension plans are being dumped, Social Security is in the tank, and our financial system is in the midst of a giant restructuring, because the stability of the past 25 years has caused prudence and what used to be called "common sense" to be set aside for greater leverage and higher risk. Retirees as well as younger investors are learning the hard way that "investing for the long term" has periods when the performance is poor and that those periods can last a decade or longer.

So, have I scared you yet? If I have, that was my intention. If you have not yet begun to invest for wealth creation, you need to start immediately, no matter what your age. If you are already investing, you need a better way to protect your money during the downturns. Now is the time to read and consider the guidance provided by Les Masonson in *Buy—DON'T Hold*. Masonson, a stock market researcher, investor, and author, has thoroughly covered all the essential bases of smart investing, and he has done so with the critical detail that is often lacking in hyped investing books written by so-called "gurus." The insights provided in this book are extremely helpful. The advice and methodology that Masonson offers throughout are useful for anyone (whether you are an investment newcomer or a longtime investor) who is interested in learning how to manage his or her investments.

My decades of experience have taught me that there are times when one should not be in the markets and are better off preserving your capital in cash equivalents because bear markets can set you back for very long periods. That is why buy-and-hold is a misguided, and often costly, investment approach. While writing and researching my book *The Complete Guide to Market Breadth Indicators*, I found that specific technical indicators are helpful in determining the changing market environment.

Additionally, the firm that I work for, Stadion Money Management, uses a proprietary technical rules-based, data-driven model to oversee the management of over $3 billion in assets in two mutual funds, separate accounts, and 401(k) plans. There are periods when these accounts are moved more into cash to protect principal. For example, in 2008 when the S&P 500 declined 37%, our Stadion Managed Fund (ETFFX with the sales load included) declined 11.22% because of our defensive approach. This fund can be invested 100% in cash if conditions dictate. Interestingly, Masonson provides an investing plan for all types of investors, with specific rules for buying and selling exchange-traded funds using a momentum-investing model based on relative strength. He first provides guidance on determining the market's overall condition using eight technical indicators so that investors are on the right side of the market. Although we use different indicators, methodologies, and ETFs, his investing approach and ours are similar in that we both strive to reduce risk and minimize losses while investing when conditions are deemed appropriate. Also, we both will exit the market and go fully into cash when the "weight of the evidence" indicates that a sell decision is warranted.

Keep in mind that the closer you get to needing your money for retirement, your children's education, or other joys of life, the worse the effect a severe bear market can have on your assets. It is critical to understand the concept of avoiding the bad markets and participating in the good markets. Masonson has offered a relatively simple approach to acquiring wealth with adequate attention to risk, and he provides the much-needed discipline to reach it. By taking the prudent advice provided in this book, you won't need luck to become a consistently profitable investor. It's never too early, or too late, to invest intelligently for your future. You have already taken the first step by reading this information-packed book. I sincerely hope that you prosper from your newly gained knowledge.

Gregory L. Morris

Gregory L. Morris is Chief Technical Analyst of Stadion Money Management, and author of *The Complete Guide to Market Breadth Indicators* and *Candlestick Charting Explained*. Previously, he served as a Trustee and advisor to the MurphyMorris ETF Fund. Greg was featured in a *BusinessWeek* article in July 2008 and was interviewed in *Technical Analysis of Stocks & Commodities* in September 2009 in an article titled "The Danger Zone with Greg Morris."

Acknowledgments

First, I'd like to thank Kenneth L. Parkinson, Managing Director of TIS Consulting, for coming up with this book's main title in about two seconds, after I mentioned the book's focus. And I'd like to thank Jerry Douma, who read my last book and profited from its guidance. He phoned and encouraged me on numerous occasions to write another book to help investors with a step-by-step method to invest more wisely. I am happy to oblige, with this book being a result of his persistence. And a special thanks to Jim Boyd, Executive Editor, and Betsy Harris, Project Editor at Pearson Education Inc. (publishing as FT Press), whom I had the pleasure to work with, and the entire publishing team involved in reviewing and delivering the final product.

As you can imagine, researching and writing an in-depth book with many facts, tables, and charts is always challenging. That being the case, I would like to thank the following individuals, firms, and Web sites for their permission to use their information in this book:

Greg Morris, Chief Technical Analyst of Stadion Money Management, for writing the foreword

George Roberts, owner, Industry Monitors and High Growth Stock Investor, and www.highgrowthstock.com for the information on this software

Mark Blake, Vice President of Sales and Marketing of VectorVest Inc. and www.vectorvest.com for the information on the VectorVest Online software program

Nathan Davis, Founder, www.etftable.com, for use of the site's ETF data on price and relative strength performance

Hugh Todd, Founder, www.etfscreen.com, for use of the site's ETF data on price and relative strength performance

Jason Goepfert, President and CEO, Sundial Capital Research, and www.SentimenTrader.com for use of the AAII Investor Sentiment chart

Chip Anderson, President, www.stockcharts.com, for the use of numerous charts from his comprehensive Web site

Doug Short and his www.dshort.com for his excellent annotated charts

Sy Harding, Editor of StreetSmartReport.com for his work on the Best Six Months Strategy with the MACD Indicator and his exhibits

Michael Johnston, Cofounder and Senior Analyst, and www.etfdb.com for information on ETF market capitalization

Michael Burke, Vice President of Institutional Training, TradeStation, for the use of three stock price charts

www.indexindicators.com for the use of one of their charts

www.etfzone.com for data on ETF net assets

And of course, I want to thank those individuals who were kind enough to provide quotes for the book jacket, including Price Headley, Jeffrey Hirsch, Robert W. Colby, Nelson Freeburg, and Paul Merriman. Lastly, I take full responsibility for any inadvertent errors or omissions.

About the Author

Leslie N. Masonson, MBA, CCM, is President of Cash Management Resources, a financial consulting firm that he founded in 1987. Masonson's 40-year working career has spanned financial advisory services, trading, investing, banking operations, management, teaching, and cash/treasury management consulting. He was also a Financial Advisor for six years offering investment services to retail clients. Earlier in his career, he worked at the large banks for a total of 17 years as a Vice President at Citibank, an Assistant Vice President at Bank of America, and an Assistant Secretary at Irving Trust Company.

He has written more than 50 articles, including interviews with traders, as well as product and book reviews for numerous financial publications, including *Technical Analysis of Stocks & Commodities, Active Trader*, and *Futures* magazine. He has lectured on investing on Crystal Cruises, Celebrity Cruise Line, and Norwegian Cruise Line. In November 2003, he was a speaker at the Intershow Online Investor's Expo, where he spoke on "Successfully Trading Stocks for a Living."

Masonson has been studying the stock market for more than 50 years. He has invested in mutual funds, stocks, options, futures, and commodities. Masonson has read more than 500 books on investing and trading, and he is proficient in technical analysis. He has used many investing and trading software programs over the years, including Telescan, OmniTrader, DTN, TradeStation, ULTRA, VectorVest, and High Growth Stock Investing, as well as many charting, investing, and trading sites on the Internet.

He has been interviewed on business radio stations, as well on cable TV on the Financial News Network and CNBC. He has been interviewed by *The Wall Street Journal, USA Today, Institutional Investor, Bottom Line/Business, Inc., Las Vegas Review-Journal*, and

Advertising Age. He has previously authored the following books: *All About Market Timing: The Easy Way to Get Started*, (McGraw-Hill, November 2003), *Day Trading On The Edge: A Look-Before-You-Leap Guide to Extreme Investing*, (AMACOM, 2000), *Cash Cash Cash: The Three Principles of Business Survival and Success*, (HarperBusiness, 1990), *Corporate Cash Management: Techniques and Analysis*, (Dow-Jones Irwin, 1985. Coedited with Frank Fabozzi), and the *Corporate Treasury Management Manual* (A.S. Pratt & Sons, 1998. Editor and Contributor).

Masonson, a permanently Certified Cash Manager (CCM), was elected to the American Management Association's "Wall of Fame" in 1989 for his contributions to teaching financial management principles to 2,600 financial managers since 1978. In addition, he has prepared and delivered training and seminars on cash management to participants at the Center for Professional Education, Treasury Management Association, Institute of Management Accountants, AICPA, Financial Executives Institute, and Healthcare Financial Management Association.

He has authored more than 50 articles on corporate cash management in the following publications: *Management Review*, *Boardroom Reports*, *Management Accounting*, *The Financial Manager*, *Chief Financial Officer USA 1988*, *Business Credit*, *Small Business Report*, *Financial Executive*, *Healthcare Financial Management*, *Investment Decisions*, *Pensions & Investment Age*, *Corporate Accounting*, and *Corporate Finance*.

Masonson received a BBA in Finance and Investments from The City College of New York and an MBA in Operations Research from Bernard M. Baruch College. His master's thesis title was "Statistical Evaluation of the Relative Strength Concept of Common Stock Selection."

Introduction

"We've got a long, long way to go before this secular bear market is over."[1]

Barry Ziskin, portfolio manager Z-Seven Fund

"For those properly prepared in advance, a bear market in stocks is not a calamity but an opportunity."

John Templeton, investor, philanthropist, mutual fund pioneer, and billionaire

My Early Beginnings in the Stock Market

In 1957, when I was 13, my interest in stock market investing was permanently set in motion. My grandmother, Dora Tuchman, gave me one share of PanAm Airways as a birthday gift. I had no idea at that time that I would be fascinated by the stock market for the rest of my life, have a 40-year banking and financial career, and have the opportunity to author three books on investing, and three books on corporate cash management.

During the 1960s and 1970s, I attended shareholder meetings in Manhattan and Brooklyn. I encountered the Gilbert brothers and Elaine Davis, shareholder activists, who challenged management in a spirited discussion of salary and perks and other relevant issues of the day.

I graduated from The City College (The City University of New York) with a BBA, majoring in Finance and Investments, and received my MBA from The Bernard M. Baruch College (The City University of New York), majoring in Operations Research. My master's thesis title was "Statistical Evaluation of the Relative Strength Concept of Common Stock Selection." I've lectured on investing on cruise ships, and I've provided guidance on mutual fund investing to friends who needed some input. From early 2004 to early 2010, I was a Financial Advisor advising clients on their investments.

My Investment Experience Spans Over 50 Years

Having studied the stock market for over 50 years, I've invested in mutual funds, stocks, options, futures, and commodities. Also, I've day traded NASDAQ stocks and E-mini-NASDAQ futures from 1998–2000 during the Internet and technology boom times. Additionally, I have read more than 500 books on investing and trading over the years, and I've become proficient in technical analysis. I've posted more than 60 financial book reviews on Amazon. Moreover, I've written investing software reviews for *Technical Analysis of Stocks & Commodities* magazine, and articles for *SFO* and *Active Trader* magazines. In addition, I've used many investing and trading software programs over the years, including Telescan, OmniTrader, DTN, TradeStation, ULTRA, VectorVest, and High Growth Stock Investor. Also, I continue to use many free charting, investing, and trading sites on the Internet.

I have subscribed to *The Wall Street Journal* and *Barron's*, and for pleasure I read many financial magazines, including *Money*, *SmartMoney*, *Forbes*, *Fortune*, and *Kiplinger's Personal Finance*. And, when I have the time, I go to my local library to read *Investor's Business Daily*, *Morningstar Mutual Funds*, *Value Line Investment*

Survey, *S&P Outlook*, and *The New York Times* business section. Over the years, I've attended many online trader expos, Money Shows, and specialized trading and investing courses. And, of course, I access useful information about investing on the Internet.

As an investor and trader, I've had successes and failures. But after many years of mixed results, I've found that mechanical non-emotional trading and investing has the highest probability of making money. In the future, I expect to not only reap more consistent returns, but also avoid bear markets. Perhaps you will follow in my footsteps and decide to use the active investing approach provided in this book or one that you develop for yourself.

I urge you to sit down and review your past investment results and determine your rate of return through today. If you are disappointed with your results for any reason, you will hopefully benefit from the approach I recommend in this book. It is critical to your investment success to find a consistent way to make money while minimizing your risk. I've concluded that buy-and-hold investing is very risky and can lead to huge losses; therefore, I've developed a more realistic, easy-to-use approach that will help you become a more consistent and more profitable investor. My goal is to provide you with the key to investment success, which is to know what to buy, when to buy, and when to sell. Profits need to be taken; otherwise, you may give them back over and over again in bear markets. That is not a smart way to manage your money. I am using the approach outlined in this book to invest my money, and I expect to have many profitable years, mainly by avoiding the bear markets and certainly by making better-than-average market returns during the bull markets.

The Purpose of This Book

My goal is to provide you with a nonemotional, systematic approach to investing that will make money in bull markets and protect your portfolio, and even make money in bear markets. This will be accomplished with a simple-to-implement strategy that has less risk than buy-and-hold because you will be out of the market during those market declines. Based on the fact that bear markets follow bull markets, if you use a buy-and-hold approach you will always lose money in bear markets. That is why you need to abandon that approach and use a proactive approach that avoids these deadly market debacles, such as the one that cost investors $11 trillion in losses during the last bear market. As an investor, you need to realize that since 1900 there have been 121 market declines of at least 10%, and 32 of these declines were 20% or more.[2]

This book provides insight about the never-ending cycle of bull and bear markets, and how to take advantage of the market's volatility. It will explain the true risks and rewards of investing, and above all provide an investing plan to sidestep the brunt of future bear markets. As a self-directed investor, you will be provided with a complete step-by-step investing approach to capture the market's upside and minimize losses, if any, when the market starts to change its trend and begin to sink. Moreover, this book provides a realistic investing approach using a time-tested strategy to first determine the market's direction based on a handful of indicators. Then after providing an appropriate universe of exchange-traded funds (ETFs) for investors of different risk levels (conservative, moderate, and aggressive) to consider, the focus shifts to using relative strength analysis to act as the filtering mechanism to select the best-performing ETFs for your investment dollars. Because ETFs have the edge in many respects, as is delineated in Chapter 4, "Exchange-Traded Funds—The Most Suitable Investment Vehicles," stocks and mutual funds are not recommended as the investment vehicles for this strategy.

Just as an airline pilot needs instrumentation to safely take off and land at the planned destination, especially during weather turbulence, investors need a reliable dashboard of instruments to maneuver through the volatile and uncertain stock market. Before the flight, the pilot reviews his or her checklist before the plane leaves the ground. Likewise, a surgeon has a protocol to follow before, during, and after operating on a patient. Similarly, as an investor you need a complete plan of action before putting your money at risk in the stock market so you know exactly when to buy and sell. Otherwise, the results could be catastrophic, similar to what could happen to a pilot or surgeon who fails to properly follow protocols and monitor the situation during the flight or surgery.

Why I Wrote This Book Now

I've met too many individuals in all age groups, who as buy-and-holders lost a large portion of their wealth by being fully invested over the past decade or just since the last market top of October 9, 2007. Unfortunately, most of them stayed fully invested based on advice from their investment advisors or based on freezing and not knowing what to do. These investors would have been better off using a strategy such as a simple moving average price crossover (for example, see the ten-month moving average chart in Figure I.1) that would have gotten them safely out of the market in November 2007, thus avoiding the entire debacle, and back in the market in June 2009 for the ride up. Hopefully, most investors decided not to sell at the March 2009 market bottom because the market then rebounded over 60% into December 2009.

Over the years I've spoken with many investors, and I've discovered that for the most part, they have a limited knowledge of investment basics, while only a small percentage really understand the key factors. That is why the majority of investors use stock brokers, financial advisors, investment professionals, and mutual fund managers. A much smaller percentage of investors manage their own money. Unfortunately, the two bear markets have interrupted many investors' plans for growing their wealth. Luckily, young people have time to recover their losses, although older individuals don't have that luxury. Most self-directed investors also took a shellacking because they were fully invested, even though they may have been well diversified. And

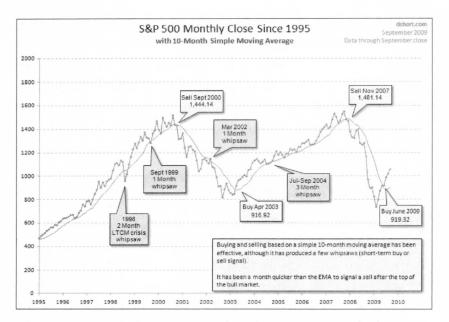

Figure I.1   S&P 500 Index with a 10-month simple moving average

Source: www.dshort.com

of course, a small percentage of self-directed investors probably did very well because they had a game plan that they followed religiously.

Just as in football, soccer, basketball, and other competitive sports, both offense and defense are needed to win games; you need the same two elements to win the investing game. With no defensive strategy you will be continually faced with the bull and bear market cycles, and you may experience no profits after decades of investing. That is not the way to build wealth.

Millions of investors have lost close to $14 trillion combined in the last two devastating bear markets this past decade. This has had devastating consequences on their lives, their families, and their futures. Investors cannot simply buy-and-hold a diversified portfolio and not look at it for 5, 10, 15, or 20 years. They may be shocked they didn't make any money at all, and after taking into account inflation and the opportunity cost of funds, they may actually come out behind. It is true that there have been no 20-year rolling periods where investors would have lost money if fully invested, but a number of those periods had very low returns—a few percent at best. Moreover, *all that matters going forward is how the markets perform over the next 20 years or more.* No one knows how that will work out from the investing perspective. That is why investors need a viable plan so that they do not repeat their mistakes of the past and possibly end up unable to retire or enjoy life to the fullest because of poor stock returns.

And that's what this book will do for you. It will show you how to read the market's overall condition, how to determine your risk level, what investing rules you need to develop, which ETFs to use, and how to put it all together to make better investment decisions, allowing you to sleep better at night.

This is a practical, easy-to-read book with an easy-to-understand investing strategy. All the data, charts, and information necessary for you to make intelligent investing decisions are readily available free on the Internet. All the key Internet sites are provided so you can get what you need. Additionally, for those of you who want more sophisticated tools, I've included a description of two user-friendly and reasonably priced software products that can provide tremendous insight into the stock market's condition with the tools and weekly commentary to take advantage of the changing market conditions.

I want to point out ahead of time that you might find that the chapters on exchange-traded funds, stock market dashboard, and relative strength somewhat intense, long, and complicated—that is not the case. It was necessary to provide you with the critical background and details so that you can easily put the recommended strategy in place. After you have worked through these chapters in particular and the remainder of the book, I'm sure you will see how easy the strategy is to set up and use on a weekly basis.

This is *not* a book about day trading or trading stocks for a living. Instead, it offers investors a road map for handling their investments in a systematic, logical, and nonemotional manner. Day trading is for those individuals who possess a certain skill set and emotional temperament to handle the stress of minute-by-minute trading. Keep in mind that day trading is extremely difficult. For those with success in other fields or a high IQ, day trading is no place to try a new profession without proper training. Otherwise, the results can be disastrous, not only financially but also emotionally. For those readers interested in determining whether day trading is for them, I refer them to my book published in 2000 as a first step, titled *Day Trading on the Edge: A Look-Before-You-Leap Guide to Extreme Investing*. It is out of print, so check your local library or used books on the Internet. Of course, there are many other more current books on the subject that provide methodologies, trading tips, and psychological pointers that you can find on Amazon or at your local book store.

Managing Your Financial Affairs Is Critical

You might be very upset and financially less well off than you were in early 2000, based on the stock market's performance over the past ten years, or even over just the past two years. This is quite understandable. With one financial mess after another, culminating in one of the worst global financial and banking crises since the 1929 depression that resulted in a bust of the housing, credit, and stock markets, the past decade has been horrific. The question is what steps you are going to take *now* to minimize your risk of potential substantial losses when the next financial meltdown or stock market crash occurs. It eventually will come—although we don't know when. We do know, based on history, that bear markets will come like clockwork to clean out your accounts, again and again. And stock market crashes arrive every 20 or 30 years, so being forewarned is being forearmed.

There is one approach that you can use that is very simple to implement: do nothing different and hope for the best. That is what most buy-and-holders do. A smarter approach is to make plans to better manage your finances and investments going forward. This book focuses on your investments. But you need to make sure that you review all aspects of your current financial situation and take the appropriate steps to put your house in order, if you have not done so already. That means budgeting; cutting expenses; saving more money; and having a will, healthcare proxy, power of attorney, and proper amount of life, health, disability, and long-term care insurance, if you can afford to pay all the premiums. And, if you have children or grandkids, make sure that you help them understand the importance of properly managing their financial matters—whether they are 8 years old, 18 years old, or older. Unfortunately, as the most recent surveys have shown, the financial literacy of our citizens is poor. And this problem needs to be urgently addressed at the public school level and beyond.

Because no one can predict where the stock market is going, why waste your money and time paying someone or some firm to baby-sit your money? More than a few top mutual fund managers have been embarrassed and humbled by the whipping their funds took in this latest bear market (for example, fund manager Bill Miller of Legg Mason Value Trust and fund manager Ronald H. Muhlenkamp of Muhlenkamp Fund, among others). And the big Ivy League endowment funds with their cadre of highly paid staff had negative performance as well.

Benefits of Managing Your Own Investments

As this book suggests, you need to immediately take control of your own investments. To help you do that, it provides a step-by-step investing approach. Here are five benefits of going this route:

- No need to subscribe to investment newsletters, magazines, or Web sites or to listen to stock tips.
- No need to listen to financial TV and radio shows to get guru recommendations.

- No need to buy load mutual funds from brokers or advisors or even no-load funds with their annual internal costs eating into performance.
- No need to buy risky individual stocks (probably after spending countless hours selecting and monitoring them or just following a guru's tip).
- No need to pay advisors 1% to 1.5% a year to manage your money. That fee eats into your performance and can amount to tens of thousands of dollars over 10 or 20 years.

Moreover, you can do the following:

- Use ETFs as your investment vehicle of choice.
- Use a low-cost discount broker to execute your trades for less than $10 each and obtain free use of their portfolio management, charting, and technical indicator software platform.
- Alter your portfolio when the market trend changes from bullish to bearish, and vice versa.
- Use the tools provided in this book to manage your investments.
- Feel confident of your ability to protect your principal even in bear markets, and sleep better at night.

After reading this book, please e-mail me your thoughts, comments, criticisms, and questions, and I'll respond. I can be reached at les@buydonthold.com. Please use the subject line "Comment on Book" in your e-mail so that I know it is not spam. I have also set up a Web site at www.buydonthold.com for additional information on the strategy presented here. If you enjoyed this book, please recommend it to friends, family members, and co-workers. The more individuals who are exposed to the approach delineated in this book, the higher the probability that they can preserve and grow their money. Be careful, be a smart investor, and be your own investment advisor. That's one way you can win the investing game.

Leslie N. Masonson
Monroe, New York
December 2009

Endnotes

1 Ziskin quoted in "Secular Bear Market Could Last into 2010, Maybe Through 2020." *Ethiopian Review*, posted July 26, 2009, by Desta Bishu.

2 Ned Davis Research as of June 30, 2009, as reported in 2009 Oppenheimer Funds *Pulse of the Market*, p. 2.

1

The Stock Market Roller Coaster

"The longer you own stocks, the greater the risk of a devastating loss."

Paul Samuelson, Nobel Laureate and author

"The time of maximum pessimism is the best time to buy and the time of maximum optimism is the best time to sell."

John Templeton, investor, philanthropist, mutual fund pioneer, and billionaire

The stock market will humble you at every opportunity, whether you are a novice or a professional investor. During bull markets, you probably tell yourself how smart you are. You may brag to family members and friends about how well your investments are perform-ing. However, in bear markets probably you tend to be withdrawn, you don't ever bring up the stock market in conversations, and you are petrified to open your brokerage and retirement fund quarterly statements.

Of course, you would love to tell everyone that you were percep-tive enough to cash out of the market near its highs, but alas, you are holding on for dear life, hoping and praying that the market rebounds as it usually does. That is how buy-and-hold investors behave in every bear market. Eventually, the stock market recovers, but no one knows how long it will take just to get back to the previous market highs. Consider the wisdom of Stan Weinstein, editor and publisher of the *Global Trend Alert* service and long-time market technician and author. When interviewed on PBS's *Nightly Business Report* on November 20, 2009, he said the following: "...to have a simple buy-and-hold strategy can be very, very dangerous for your investing health and wealth." As you will see in future chapters, he is absolutely right.

Secular Bull and Bear Markets

Historically, since 1871 there have been six long-term (secular) bull and bear markets. As you can see in the chart shown in Figure 1.1, which is adjusted for inflation, the percentage gains in the bull markets range between 266% and 666%, whereas the bear markets have lost between 54% and 81%. Therefore, it is very important to try to protect your principal from the devastation caused by these long-term bear markets.

Figure 1.1   S&P 500 secular bull and bear markets

Source: dshort.com

Latest Bear Market

The October 9, 2007, to March 9, 2009, bear market was one of the worst in history. As of October 20, 2009, the S&P 500 Index was still 30.3% below its prior peak. The chart shown in Figure 1.2 provides a view of this bear market, which includes four rallies ranging in magnitude from 7.4% to 24.2% that were followed by five downward moves. Some investors reentered the market on these rallies only to be further battered. That is why investors need an action plan on how to handle their investments on a more methodical and less emotional basis. This latest bear market is only the latest in a long history of market declines, as covered in more detail in the next section.

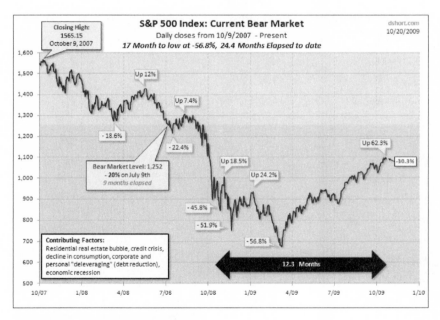

Figure 1.2   The last bear market

Source: dshort.com

Bear Markets Have a Long Recovery Time

Table 1.1 shows how long it takes to get back to prior highs in bull markets from the bear market lows. Excluding the outlier data from the 1929 crash, it took an average of 3.8 years to get back to the prior bull market high. However, after the 2000–2002 bear market you had to wait 7 years to get back even with an all-stock portfolio. If you owned just a tech stock portfolio, you are not even close to breaking even, and you were still 60% below the peak in March 2002 when the NASDAQ Composite hit 5084.

TABLE 1.1   A Bear Market Break-Even Analysis Based on S&P 500 Index

Bear Market Period	Duration (Months)	% Decline	Years to Break Even
Sept. '29–June '32	33	86.7	25.2
July '33–Mar. '35	20	33.9	2.3
Mar. '37–Mar. '38	12	54.5	8.8
Nov. '38–Apr. '42	41	45.8	6.4
May '46–Mar. '48	22	28.1	4.1
Aug. '56–Oct. '57	14	21.6	2.1
Dec. '61–June '62	6	28.0	1.8
Feb. '66–Oct. '66	8	22.2	1.4
Nov. '68–May '70	18	36.1	3.3
Jan. '73–Oct. '74	21	48.2	7.6
Nov. '80–Aug. '82	21	27.1	2.1
Aug. '87–Dec. '87	4	33.5	1.9
July '90–Oct. '90	3	19.9	0.6
Mar. '00–Oct. '02	31	49.1	7.0
Oct. '07–Mar. '09	18	56.7	TBD

Historical Market Returns Are Not a Forecast of Future Returns

You need to understand that investing for the long term is an aggregation of multiple short-term time frames. If you don't invest well in the short-term periods, your long-term results will suffer. Unfortunately, no one knows in advance the direction of the stock market over any time frame. So it is critical that you find and use an investing approach that grows your money within your personal risk parameters, and, more important than that, provides a warning of an impending change in market direction that could turn into another bear market.

According to Morningstar,[1] the average annual return from 1926 through 2008 of three well-known asset classes was as follows:

> Cash (measured by 30-day T-bill): 3.7%
>
> Long-term bonds (Ibbotson Associates Long-Term Government Bond Index): 5.7%
>
> Large Stocks (S&P 500 Index): 9.6%

Keep in mind that these results are just averages, and they don't imply that you will be able to replicate these returns over your personal investment time horizon. No one has a clue as to the stock market's future performance, so don't waste your time listening to predictions of Wall Street prognosticators because your guess is as good as theirs. Unbelievably, according to the Leuthold Group, U.S. T-bonds performed better than stocks for the past 10-, 20-, and 30-year periods.[2] During this time frame, investors owning bonds or bond funds had higher returns with less market risk than those owning stocks. That's how nutty the risk versus return equation has become.

Forget About Relying on Investment Books with Outrageous Titles

Do you remember the book that came out on November 14, 2000, titled *Dow 36,000: The New Strategy for Profiting from the Coming Rise in the Stock Market,* by James K. Glassman and Kevin A. Hassett? They predicted that the Dow would reach that level in three to ten years. Well, that didn't happen, did it? In the authors' media appearances, I understand that they were saying things such as "the time to get in the market is now and don't be a fool and miss this great opportunity to invest." Unfortunately, some investors heeded their advice and lost a bundle.

Another more outrageous book, published on June 26, 1999, titled *Dow 40,000: Strategies for Profiting from the Greatest Bull Market in History,* by David Elias, slightly missed the mark as well. He predicted that the Dow would achieve 40,000 by 2016. He still has a shot at being right, but the probability is almost nil. After hitting 11,125.13 on April 12, 2000, the Dow didn't reach that level again until early 2006. After hitting an all-time peak of 14,164.53 on October 9, 2007, the Dow cratered to 6547.05 on March 9, 2009, and touched 10,500 as of December 1, 2009. But it is still 25.9% lower than its 2007 high.

Stock Market Facts

Before beginning our journey to providing a sound investing approach that focuses on offense and defense, let's start with some indisputable facts about the stock market:

1. Since 1929, there have been 15 bear markets, averaging 20 months in length with an average decline of 39.4%. Leaving out the 1929 crash, the average decline was still 36%. The last two bear markets were among the worst ever, dropping 49.1% and

56.7%, respectively. Bull markets occur about 70% of the time, and bear markets occur about 30% of the time. A bear market has occurred every three to four years since 1900 with average declines of about 30%. The bear markets in 1987, 1990, and 1998 were the shortest, while the 1973–1974, 2000–2002, and 2007–2009 bear markets were the most devastating. So bear markets are frequent and the damage they can inflict in investor portfolios is severe.

2. No one can consistently predict the market's future direction or performance with any degree of reliability. Of course, there have been isolated impressive stock crash calls by gurus in past years, but they failed to deliver on future calls. Moreover, each call was by a different guru. For example, the bear market calls of Marty Zweig and Elaine Garzarelli before the 1987 crash and Joe Granville's call in the early 1970s were prescient. In early March 2009, Doug Kass of Seabreeze Partners said on CNBC that the generational stock market low for the year would occur within a few days, and he was correct. However, he also said previously that a low was at hand on earlier dates, but this time he was more definitive. He also called a market top for the year on August 26 for the rest of the year. As of December 4, 2009, he was wrong, as the market was approaching a high for the year.

3. Stock market history provides a perspective on what has happened in the past, but tells nothing about what to expect in the future. Just because the *stock market returned an average of 9.6% from 1926 to 2008*, going forward that provides no clue as to what the next few years or decades will bring. The best decades were the 1950s, with an average annual return of 19%, followed by the 1980s and 1990s at about 18% per year on average. The decade of 2000, where the market dropped an average of about 1.6% based on the S&P 500 Index through December 1, 2009, will be the worst decade, even worse than

the 1930s. Sometimes the market does nothing for extended periods. Interestingly, during this decade, the MSCI Emerging Markets Index jumped an average of 8.2% a year. So you have to be on the lookout for leading markets. Look at the chart shown in Figure 1.3, which shows the lack of progress over 23 years in the Dow-Jones Industrial Average.

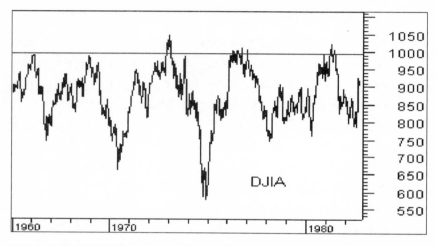

Figure 1.3   The U.S. stock market, 1960s through early 1980s

Source: StreetSmartReport. Printed with permission

4. Buying-and-holding a diversified basket of 10 or 20 individual stocks is typically more risky than buying an index fund of the entire stock market, such as the Vanguard Total Stock Market (VTI) exchange-traded fund, because the risk is spread across thousands of stocks rather than a small number of stocks.

5. In bear markets, buy-and-holders lose money. In 2008, even with a diversified portfolio, investors had big losses. In most cases, a diversified portfolio of stocks and bonds (or mutual funds) provides a cushion against the drop, but the overall annual portfolio performance may still be negative. Even with a broadly based portfolio with a common mix of 60% stocks/40%

bonds in 2008, using the Vanguard Total Stock Market (–37.04% total return) and Total Bond Market (+5.05%) ETFs as broad market indicators, their combined total return was –20.2%.

6. The larger the losses investors incur in a bear market, the longer it takes and the harder it is to get back even. For example, if investors lose 40% of their portfolio value in a deep bear market, say losing $40,000 on a $100,000 portfolio, then they will need a rise of $40,000, or 66.67%, in the portfolio to get back even. A percentage rise of this magnitude will typically take years to occur. Amazingly, a return of almost this magnitude occurred from March 9, 2009, through early December 2009 in many stock mutual funds, ETFs, and individual securities. This substantial return in such a short period is very rare and should not be considered the return of the roaring bull market of the 1980s and 1990s. It was simply a rebound from very depressed levels.

Arguments For and Against Buy-and-Hold (BAH)

The buy-and-hold investing approach has been around for over 50 years. That by itself does not mean that it is the best approach for the ordinary investor. So let's review the arguments for and against it.

Ten Arguments for BAH

1. Over the long run stocks have the best overall return compared to bonds, treasury bills, and cash; thus, buying stocks is the only way to stay ahead of inflation.

2. A diversified portfolio of individual stocks and bonds and broad-based mutual funds will provide positive returns over long time frames.

3. Since no one can predict the future performance of the stock market, it pays to stay fully invested all the time.

4. The stock market has always recovered from bear markets and gone onto new highs, so patience pays.

5. When investors miss out on the ten best days, weeks, or months, their stock market returns are greatly diminished. Since no one knows when these instances will occur, it is best to be invested all the time so you are always invested for the best periods.

6. Over the long term, trying to trade and pick the high and low points of the market to sell and buy, respectively, doesn't work, and no one can accomplish that feat consistently. Also, commissions and taxes will eat away at the principal.

7. There are no additional commission costs after the initial purchase of a stock portfolio or load mutual funds as it is kept for the long term.

8. Investors can buy no-load active and/or passive (index funds) directly from many fund families and not pay commissions.

9. Rebalancing the portfolio (whether stocks, bonds, or mutual funds) once a year to the desired level of stocks vs. bonds (for example, 60% stocks/40% bonds) will typically improve performance over time as profitable investments are sold and less-well-acting investments are bought. This is best done in retirement accounts since there are no tax consequences, whereas in regular brokerage or mutual fund accounts, every sale will constitute a taxable event, either short- or long-term.

10. Taxes are nonexistent on stock purchases until they are sold. However, mutual funds do pass on capital gains at year-end. They are paid automatically to investors who must pay tax for that tax year in their regular brokerage account. Their retirement accounts are not impacted by these annual distributions from a tax perspective.

Seven Arguments Against BAH

1. You need at least a 20-year time horizon to ensure that you come out ahead, *but* there have been a number of 20-year rolling periods during which the stock market performance was very weak or negative if you factor in inflation.

2. An investor is exposed to all bear markets and crashes (black swans). If you never take profits, you may keep giving them back time and again—just look at the yo-yo market from the peak in the first quarter of 2000 to the market bottom on October 9, 2002, to the next peak on October 9, 2007, to the market bottom on March 6, 2009.

3. No headway was made by the vast majority of buy-and-hold investors who were invested since 1998 through 2009. After taking into account inflation, many investors were way behind in their retirement and 529 college savings plans for their college-bound children and grandkids.

4. Even asset diversification failed to provide positive results in 2008, as it was did in prior bear markets, during which certain asset classes had positive returns. All asset classes in the 2008 bear market cratered except long-term treasury bond funds and ETFs, and cash (and U.S. Government and U.S. Treasury money market funds were yielding 0% interest for months—not a way to beat inflation).

5. BAH does not have a defensive mechanism; therefore, it offers no value in a bear market. BAH is feasible only when the stock market rises, but we know that 30% of the years are down years. Moreover, if the stock market's drawdown (percent decline from a market peak to its trough) was a maximum of 10% or less, then the majority of investors would probably be able to stomach those drops knowing that they could make easily their money back in the next bull run. *However*, that is not the case,

and actually market drawdowns occur frequently (40% of the time) and the average drawdown is –18%, if the 1929 crash drawdown of 85% is not included. In the latest bear market the drawdown was –56.7% using the S&P 500 Index (October 9, 2007, price of 1565 compared to 677 on March 9, 2009).

6. Missing the worst days, weeks, or months in the market is much preferred to missing the best days, weeks, or months. Numerous studies have shown this to be the case. In any event, this entire argument is bogus since no one will consistently miss the best or worst periods. The buy-and-hold crowd just wants to scare investors by demonstrating that missing the best days hurts their returns. *However*, they never include the counterargument that contradicts their flawed logic. That shows the bias of mutual funds and investment managers who keep putting forth their partial statistics.

7. Commissions for buying and selling stocks or ETFs have dropped significantly in the past few years. Using a discount broker, an investor can pay as little as $1 a trade, and in many cases less than $10. Thus, commissions are not really a cost-prohibitive factor to worry about for the average investor. However, day traders have to take into account their commissions as these costs mount up quickly.

Mutual Fund Managers Do Not Practice Buy-and-Hold

Mutual fund managers earn higher fees when the assets they manage grow and vice versa. Assets under management (AUM) is the key factor that drives the funds to keep the buy-and-hold mantra alive and well. Interestingly, mutual fund managers do not buy and hold, so why should you? If the BAH strategy were so worthwhile, then these managers would use it themselves and not trade their portfolios so often. According to *Morningstar Mutual Funds* (October 24, 2009, issue), the portfolio turnover rates for different types of mutual funds were as follows:

Domestic Stock	97%
International Stock	85%
Specialty (sector)	159%
Balanced	69%
Specialty Bond	88%
General Bond	178%
Government Bond	333%
Municipal Bond	32%

Would you have ever guessed that in the staid asset class of bonds the annual portfolio turnover was over 100% for two of the four categories? In general, that means that during a 12-month period they replaced every bond in the portfolio with another bond. Believe it or not, the annual turnover for government bonds was 333%. This high turnover results in added transaction costs and bid-ask spread costs that are imbedded into the net asset value and reduce overall investor returns. Also, this translates into capital gains that are distributed to shareholders each year, even though the shareholder did not sell the fund. Sometimes there are capital losses, and they are used to offset the gains over time. The mutual fund company can carry the excess losses from one year forward for years to offset against gains. Investors who buy the fund will benefit from those losses until they run out.

Not only don't mutual funds practice buy-and-hold, but also they have raised their annual average expense ratios compared to a year earlier. Their current ratio is 1.5%. Over 70% of stock mutual funds have increased this fee by 0.082 of a percentage point, whereas the remainder raised them by 0.1 percent. This equates to $1 million in added revenue to a $10 billion fund. Interestingly, the fee for sector funds was raised the most at 0.109 percentage points. Bond fund ratios remained flat. The main reason for these increases in the expense ratios was the fall in fund prices, as the funds encountered a reduction in their asset base, resulting in a 40% drop in revenue from November 2008 through June 2009.[3]

Wall Street's Objective Is to Keep Your Money Under Management

Basically, Wall Street wants you to believe that investing not only is complicated and difficult to do successfully on your own, but also requires special expertise that you don't have or don't have the time or interest to learn. Wall Street says to just buy-and-hold a diversified portfolio of stocks and bonds or mutual funds, rebalance yearly, and sit back and watch your nest egg grow decade after decade. This is a nice fable if you live in Disney's Fantasyland. Unfortunately, for the vast majority of investors this advice has been not only wrong, but extremely costly for the past decade.

Not all 10- and 15-year rolling periods have been able to provide the long-term average return of 9.6%, with a fair number of those periods well below that number. Although all 20-year rolling periods (for example, 1961–1980, 1962–1981, etc.) have had positive stock market returns, they are widely dispersed as to the range of returns, with a number of those periods returning only 2% to 3%. Moreover, after inflation is taken into account, there were negative years. Also a 20-year time horizon or longer may not be representative of your or other investors' time frames due to age, income, and life-changing situations. John Maudlin, an analyst, commentator, and author, analyzed 88 20-year periods and found that 50% produced compounded annual returns of less than 4%, while less than 10% generated gains of more than 10%.

In the Stock Market Expect the Unexpected

Unfortunately, natural and man-made disasters can occur on a huge scale without warning. Massive destruction of property and life can result, and it usually takes many years to recover, if at all. As an example, just consider how catastrophic Hurricane Katrina impacted the housing, employment, and everyday life of New Orleans residents. There is a parallel to investing in the stock market. Severe bear markets and stock market crashes have occurred throughout history and will likely occur again in the future. Individual investors who do not have a predetermined defensive investing plan will take big hits to their portfolios, and many investors will not have the time to recover their losses due to age, sickness, loss of jobs, home foreclosures, and other unforeseen factors. That is why just sitting back and not paying attention to changing conditions is dangerous to your wealth and health.

Three Reasons for Corrections, Crashes, and Bear Markets

There are many financial, economic, and political reasons for corrections and crashes. Among the most common reasons are the following:

1. *Euphoria and overvaluation*—Markets get overheated and the public can't buy stocks fast enough. This leads to disastrous consequences, such as the infamous Crash of October 1929, with the ensuing drop of 89% in stock market values when the market bottomed in 1932. Similarly, the technology and Internet bubble in 2000 resulted in crushing blows to many high-flying Internet companies that lost over 90% of their value,

merged, or went bankrupt. And the financial meltdown in 2008 and the first quarter of 2009 resulted in huge losses at big banks and investment banks. Lehman Brothers went bankrupt and JPMorgan Chase absorbed Bear Stearns and Washington Mutual. Moreover, there were millions of mortgage delinquencies, the housing market collapsed and housing prices fell across the country, there were huge government bailouts, over six million people were unemployed, hundreds of car dealerships closed, and there was a worldwide impact of the crisis. No wonder the stock market got crushed.

2. *Leveraging assets*—Stock margin buying in the Crash of 1929 added to the panic and stock prices fell further as margin calls to individual investors went unanswered. Highly leveraged mortgage securities and other financial instrument failures resulted in the Crash of 2008. These toxic securities and their worldwide distribution to investors and institutions turned out to be the death knell of the markets, and especially the financial stocks—banks, insurance companies, investment banks. This led to a worldwide financial crisis and a loss of confidence in the financial and banking systems, as well as the U.S. government.

3. *Decreased company earnings*—Decreased earnings translate into lower share prices, recessions, and depressions. Companies close, file for bankruptcy protection, merge, or try to survive. Millions of workers are laid off and consumer spending is adversely affected, resulting in additional cutbacks in other sectors of the economy—travel, housing, restaurants, retail stores, and so forth.

Market Crashes Are Devastating

Financial advisors, brokerage firms, mutual fund companies, and institutions continue to push the buy-and-hold mantra that has totally failed investors twice within the past ten years, and many times since

1900. Take a look the horrendous performance of the major averages shown in Table 1.2.

TABLE 1.2   The Last Two Crushing Bear Markets

Index	10/9/02, Low	Percent Change (1)	10/9/07, High	3/9/09, Low	Percent Change
Dow Jones Industrials	7286.27	–37.8	14,164.53	6,547.05	–53.7
S&P 500	776.76	–49.1	1,565.18	676.53	–56.7
NASDAQ Composite	1114.11	–77.9	2,859.12°	1,268.64	–55.6

°October 31, 2007

1. Percent change from March 2000 highs (S&P and NASDAQ) and from January 14, 2000, for Dow-Jones Industrials

Time to Break Even After Bear Market Debacle

How long does it take to get back even on big losses in these two bear markets? Just look at Table 1.3 to find out.

TABLE 1.3   The Percentage Returns Required to Break Even

Bear Market Loss	Three-Year Returns	Five-Year Returns	Seven-Year Returns
–10%	3.6%	2.1%	1.5%
–30%	12.6%	7.4%	5.2%
–50%	26.0%	14.9%	10.4%
–60%	35.7%	20.1%	14.0%

A 50% loss in one year, first of all, requires a 100% return just to break even. For example, a stock or mutual fund that you bought for $25 per share would be priced at $12.50 if it fell 50%. Then, if it increased in price back to $25, that would be a 100% increase. Now, assuming that the stock goes up 10.4% a year for the next seven years, that will bring you back even. Of course, if the stock goes up only 7.2% a year (not shown), it will take ten years to get back to even. As you can see, the larger your loss, the longer it may take to get even.

It took until 2007 for the peak of the 2000 market to be reached again. If you had stayed fully invested and waited for the bear market to recover, you not only had a big drawdown of your principal of nearly 50%, but gave up an "opportunity cost" of funds. During that time, you could have been safely earning interest with your principal intact, if you had gone into cash or cash equivalents when the market started turning down in March 2000. Not only would you have earned decent interest averaging about 3% to 5%, but 100% of your principal would have been safe waiting for the next entry point. That is a phenomenal position to be in. You are probably saying to yourself that no one can be that good on their timing, but you'd be wrong, as we will demonstrate with our strategy.

Secular Bear Markets Are Not That Rare

A secular bear market is a flat or declining price trend that lasts many years during which the market meanders, with intermittent bear market short cycles and a number of substantial but unsustainable bull market rallies. Three secular bear markets have occurred since 1900:

- 1906–1921
- 1929–1949
- 1966–1982
- 2000–? (2015 to 2020, perhaps)

We may be in the fourth secular bear market right now, but we will not know for a number of years. As of year-end 2009, the market has not breached its highs of October 2007. Thus, from early 2000 through 2009, we have been in a secular bear market—that's now ten years and counting.

In March through December 2009, as the market was still charging ahead, there was constant discussion on CNBC, on Bloomberg radio, and in the financial media as to whether this historic rise in such a short time was the beginning of a secular (long-term) bull market or just a cyclical (short-term) bull market in the secular bear market that began in 2000. First of all, no one can know the answer to that question until well after the fact. Second, who cares what the experts' opinions are because they are no better than your guess or mine, and the experts disagree with each other—you shouldn't make investment decisions based on this blather. Third, if you have a systematic investment approach, like the one presented in this book, then you don't have to waste your time listening to, watching, or reading about this useless debate.

Investing in the Stock Market Is a Very Risky Proposition

From the last October 9, 2007, market high to the crash low of March 9, 2009, investors lost an estimated $11 trillion of market value. Those investors who sold out at or near the March lows or before benefiting from the 60%+ rally into year-end 2009 took a financial shellacking. Even with this unexpected huge short-term rally, most broad stock market averages were still about 25% to 30% below the prior peak. Once a severe market drop occurs, it can take many years to get back even. Because of the possibility of future crushing market meltdowns, investors need to understand that investing in the stock market is a very risky proposition, no matter what anyone tells them to the contrary.

As examples of risky stocks, consider the number of "supposed" blue-chip companies that have gone bankrupt, have merged, have been taken over, or have seen their share prices drop to single digits in recent years. This should be a clear sign to investors that nothing is guaranteed to last forever and that individual companies can go bust if there is inept management, accounting or financial scandals, or outside factors impacting their ability to make a profit. Even the well-known Dow Jones Industrial Average has had to replace various stocks over the years due to poor financial performance or mergers.

In today's interconnected fast-moving digital global economy, investing successfully is a big challenge compared to prior decades.

At any instant in time, the combined knowledge of all investors—professional and amateur—is baked into the price of a stock. As news about a stock or major event hits the airwaves—the Internet, cable TV, cellphones, Blackberries, iPhones, and now Twitter—the information is quickly spread across the globe in seconds. This instant communication immediately impacts the stock price and investors can see the price action on the fly. Of course, rumors and false information spread just as quickly and can knock down a stock price even though the drop is not warranted. Investing in individual stocks is extremely risky as any negative news can knock down the price 25% in seconds. A portfolio of stocks will reduce the overall risk, but if the whole market declines, the odds are high that your portfolio will decline as well.

Market players around the globe—institutions, pension funds, money management firms, banks, endowments, hedge funds, speculators, and individuals—are causing more price volatility, resulting in a changing playing field. Individual investors need to have a well-thought-out game plan with proper risk controls to mitigate potential bad investment decisions. Unfortunately, most investors have no written game plan, no investing rules as to what to buy, when to buy, or when to sell. This lack of preparation can result in unnecessary large losses resulting in great emotional and financial pain.

Investing in certain stocks based on a stock "tip," or not assessing when to invest, is a major shortfall of most investors. On the surface, it may appear that any time is opportune for investments, since individual stocks move up and down all the time, and stock market gurus put forth the premise that no one can time the market. But this premise is false. There is a time to be invested and there is a time to be safely in cash. Just think about the past ten years and ask yourself whether having a cash position during the two severe market collapses would have been preferable to being fully invested and then waiting patiently and nervously for the market to rebound.

Preservation of Capital Is Paramount

Preservation of capital is the key component of any investing plan. You must have a plan to protect your money as the market trend turns downward; otherwise, you will have to sit through painful periods of market decline. Astute investors welcome markets moving in sustained up and down trends, as they can make money by riding the stock market roller coaster, investing long and short, respectively. However, for ordinary investors down markets cause panic and incorrect emotional decision making. More often than not, these uninformed investors *sell* at market *bottoms*, and *buy* at market *tops*, thereby unintentionally destroying their chances of making back their losses on the market's eventual recovery.

A 2008 Phoenix Wealth Survey of high-net-worth baby boomers found that 41% are now making their own investment decisions because they did not feel that their financial advisors' advice or fees were helping their portfolio performance. Moreover, about 35% of boomers have a formal written financial plan, but they may not pay attention to it during boom times, but only when things get bad.[4] Moreover, after the crushing returns in this most recent bear market, investors have been left with only a handful of options to recover their losses, including investing more aggressively, reducing their expenses, saving more money, continuing to work, and reducing their purchases of discretionary items such as restaurant meals, movies, vacations, travel, and new cars. Amazingly, almost 70% of boomers claim to be financially unprepared for retirement.

Investors were not the only stock market losers in 2008 and early 2009. Hedge funds lost an average of 18%, and many pension funds and endowment funds encountered huge investment losses. In the fiscal year ending June 2009, Yale, Harvard, and Princeton lost about 25% of their endowments, and CalPERS (California Public Employees' Retirement System), the country's biggest pension fund, had preliminary losses of 23.4% or a staggering $56 billion from the previous year-end value of $180.9 billion. Likewise, the California State Teachers' Retirement System lost about 25% or $43 billion from its previous asset base of $118.8 billion.[5] Warren Buffett, one of the most successful, most well-known, and shrewdest investors of all time, was not immune from the financial crisis and stock market mauling, as Berkshire Hathaway's Class A share price fell 53.4%, dropping from a lofty peak of $148,900 on December 11, 2007, to a low of $73,195 on March 9, 2009.

Goldman Sachs, a very sophisticated investment firm, uses high-frequency (trading millions of shares) automated trading software programs based on predetermined formulas that buy and sell securities globally. During the week of July 3, 2009, for example, the firm was responsible for almost 25% of the programmed trading on the NYSE, making it the number-one-ranked player. Currently, it is estimated that high-frequency trading accounts for approximately 75% of U.S. stock trading in 2009 through mid-July, compared to 59% in 2008. Amazingly, this strategy made money for its astute players in 2008 when other strategies got clobbered.[6] There is much more automated computerized trading by some big players, which can change the market direction in an instant and cause unexpected volatility. In 2008, for example, the stock market was more volatile than at any time since the end of the stock market crash ending in 1932. The S&P 500 Index either gained or lost more than 3% a day 42 times during that year, compared to 5 such occurrences in the prior five years.

Now that you understand that bear markets follow bull markets and that severe losses can damage your portfolio for years to come, the next step is for you to really understand the risk you take when you invest. Especially after your stock market experience over the past few years, you may find that you really didn't understand how risky investing could be. That is why the next chapter is devoted to understanding risk.

Endnotes

1 Personal Recovery Guide (The Hartford) 2009.

2 Farzad, Robert. "Searching the Stock Market for True North." *BusinessWeek*, October 5, 2009.

3 Waggoner, John, "Funds' expense ratios are rising." *USA Today*, November 13, 2009.

4 "High-Net-Worth Boomers Ditch the Advice." *Boomer Market Advisor*, November 2008, p. 17.

5 Karmin, Craig. "Calpers Has Worst Year, Off 23.4%." *The Wall Street Journal*, July 22, 2009.

6 Patterson, Scott. "Rivals Play Catch-Up as Goldman Thrives." *The Wall Street Journal*, July 13, 2009.

2

Understanding the Concept of Risk

"Risk comes from not knowing what you're doing."
Warren Buffett

"Risk is good. Not properly managing your risk is a dangerous leap."
Evel Knievel, motorcyclist

Risk is part of everyday life. Whether you cross the street, drive a car or motorcycle, take an airplane flight, eat in a restaurant, or invest in the stock market, there are risks involved—some small and some large. Actually, almost everything you do has some degree of risk associated with it. So it is important that you understand the risks of investing before you find out the hard way that you didn't pay as much attention as you should have, and you now have stock market losses beyond what you can afford. And possibly the losses are so large that your future life goals are in jeopardy of being unfulfilled.

Do you have a plan for achieving your financial goals, especially managing your investments? By keeping your money in CDs and money market accounts, you will find that the growth needed to counter inflation will not be possible, especially since interest rates are at record lows and taxes are due on investment income, if it is not a retirement account. As an investor, you need to establish a risk level, and then make sure that you don't make bets that are not in line with this level.

Factors that typically enter the risk tolerance equation include age, current income, marital situation, number of dependents, expenses, savings, expected large expenditures, life expectancy, number of years of continued employment, time frame for retirement account accumulation and distribution phases, and current value of retirement and regular brokerage accounts.

Risk Tolerance Questionnaires Have Major Shortcomings

As an investor, you need to carefully determine your "risk versus reward" parameters. Your challenge is to make sure that you balance risk and reward to suit your particular financial situation. You need to understand that only after actually experiencing a severe market decline will you be able to pinpoint your "real" risk tolerance. Most financial institutions and brokerage firms use a simple one-page risk tolerance questionnaire with about ten questions to assess an investor's risk tolerance.

Unfortunately, the actual questions and response choices are not that realistic and do not provide you or the advisor with your "real" risk tolerance. The key question that needs to be answered by you is "At what percent decline in stock market value will you give up and say to sell?" Another name for that amount is *maximum drawdown*. Assessing your risk by completing a risk tolerance questionnaire while sitting comfortably in a broker's office and opening an account is quite a different situation from actually living through the nightmare of your portfolio cratering 50% in 18 months. If you have been investing since 1998 and certainly afterward, you have most likely seen no gain in your portfolios. I'm sure that's not exactly what you had in mind when you invested your money.

Typical Risk Tolerance Questions

Following are some examples of risk tolerance questions from typical brokerage firm and advisory services:

1. Which best describes your investment objective?
2. What is your investment time horizon?
3. How old are you?
4. How important is it for your portfolio to generate income?
5. Do you know that there is no such thing as risk-free investment?
6. How willing are you to accept fluctuations in the value of your portfolio?
7. What annual total return are you looking for over your investing period?
8. How much does the market have to fall before you'll sell a portion or a percentage of your holdings?
9. If your portfolio dropped 50% in value, what would you do?
10. If you agreed to a specific investment plan, what is the probability that you would stick with it over bull and bear market cycles?
11. How important is it to be able to liquidate your portfolio with little loss of principal?
12. How willing are you to accept short-term losses if your investment horizon is long-term (over 20 years)?
13. How extensive is your investment knowledge?
14. Would you be described as a risk taker or risk avoider?

Each question typically provides three to five choices for answers. After you complete this questionnaire, each answer is given a certain numeric weight and then tallied by the broker or advisor for your total score. The lowest scores are placed in the "conservative" investor category, while the highest are considered "aggressive" investors. Average scores result in a "moderate" investor classification. You are then provided with a suggested portfolio allocation, such as 40% stocks/60% bonds for conservative investors, 60% stocks/40% bonds for moderate investors, and 80% stocks/20% bonds (or 100% stocks) for aggressive investors.

The problem with these neatly packaged allocations is that they do not take into account whether stocks or bonds will be the better-performing asset class over the next year, five years, or longer or whether your risk assessment is accurate. You would be better served by being more heavily weighted in the best performing asset classes. When any of the current asset classes lose price momentum, the portfolio can be adjusted and switched into a more strongly performing class. As explained in Chapter 6, "Using Relative Strength Analysis to Determine Where to Invest," that can be accomplished by using the relative strength approach that pinpoints the best-performing asset classes. Using such a mechanical trading approach will help you avoid a desire to chase the hot funds or stocks of the day. The key to successful investing is to take your emotions out of the equation. That is why a step-by-step action plan is presented in Chapter 3, "Personal Investing Plan: Six-Step Road Map to Success." You need a specific, logical approach to managing your investments so that you meet your goals.

New Risk Tolerance Questionnaires

There have been positive developments in redesigning risk tolerance questionnaires based on the findings of behavioral finance studies of investors. By going to Google and typing in "risk tolerance questionnaire," you should be able to come up with some interesting and useful sites to determine your personal risk tolerance.

For example, a number of articles have been written on determining an individual's attitude toward risk by using a psychometric profile.[1] This profile analyzes an individual's intelligence, personality traits, and aptitude. Currently, it is more heavily used in assessing an individual's reading and math skills. Psychometric risk tolerance questionnaires attempt to measure an investor's risk tolerance (how an investor perceives risk) compared to his or her risk capacity (amount of risk an investor can afford to take).

FinaMetrica Questionnaires

FinaMetrica Pty Ltd is a firm that provides this type of questionnaire to its clients (financial advisors and individuals) with a detailed report on their findings dubbed, "Personal Financial Risk Profile." The firm has developed a 25-item multiple-choice questionnaire so that the results are statistically significant and because fewer questions do not provide sufficient insight into the investor's psyche. Most questions have four to five choices, thereby providing the individual with more options that fit his or her situation. Their report provides a numeric score of an individual's risk compared to a bell curve showing seven risk groups, your score, and the percentage of individuals in that scoring range from past data collection. The key areas covered include your risk tolerance score, your risk group, your ability to make financial decisions, how you handle financial disappointments, your financial past, your expected investment portfolio return, tax advantages on your investments, and your handling of borrowed money.

Other organizations that have developed new versions of their risk tolerance questionnaires are Assessment Service, based in New York, and Barclays Wealth.[2]

I was able to take advantage of a free offer to fill out a FinaMetrica questionnaire and obtain their report on my risk profile. I found the results accurate and enlightening. For further information on their offerings, go to www.finametrica.com or www.riskprofiling.com.

Recent Market Decline Has Brought Risk to the Forefront

Do you really understand stock market risk? Wouldn't you want to earn a 10% or more annual return on your investments with little or no risk? Unfortunately, that combination of variables does not exist in the real world. The key is to ask yourself how much you can afford to lose, rather than how much you hope to gain. Focus more on downside protection than on upside projection. You need the proper mind-set. That means not only playing market offense, but, more importantly, playing market defense.

As an investor, you need to use defense so that you will have more money on the table over your lifetime. This is the opposite approach of that used by the uninvolved buy-and-holders who hope and pray that the market will rise during their investment time horizon, and especially in the later years when they need to withdraw the funds to live on or pass on.

What has really brought the subject of risk to the forefront was the huge 57% decline in the S&P 500 Index impacting all asset classes during the 18-month bear market bottoming on March 9, 2009. There was no place to hide, except for treasury bonds and cash equivalents. Investors who sold out at or near the market bottom quickly learned about their risk tolerance. Based on the market volatility and their investment losses piling up in 2008, investors need to reevaluate their "true" risk tolerance. Even "conservative" investors with a 40% stock/60% bond portfolio took a beating in this bear market.

As an investor, you should sit down and ask yourself, "What risk do I want to take going forward?" Then when that level is determined, you need to bake that risk level into your investing plan and make sure that you have a way to protect against a decline that could wipe you out. (An investing plan for your consideration is presented in Chapter 3.) Now let's cover the risks you encounter as an investor.

Market and Individual Stock Risk

Investing in stocks and bonds entails risk, perhaps more risk than you are aware of. From 1926 to 2008, the stock market, as measured by the S&P 500 Index, posted negative returns 24 times in 83 years (28.9% of the time). Since you cannot forecast the bad years ahead of time, one option to consider is to buy-and-hold where you hope to survive the down years. But by not taking any defensive action to protect your capital, you are not using a rational investing approach.

Moreover, buying individual stocks is more risky than owning a stock mutual fund. Investing in individual stocks is more risky than investing in treasury bills, but the rewards should be greater. However, the returns on stocks have been negative over this past decade, and the earnings in T-bills have been positive. Investing in a U.S. Treasury bond fund is usually less risky than investing in a corporate bond fund, since the probability of a corporation failing and not being able to pay back bondholders is higher than the probability of the U.S. Government failing to pay back the principal of their bond. However, the price of the U.S. Treasury bond fund, especially the 30-year bond, sometimes is more volatile than that of corporate bonds and also offers a lower yield. In some situations your understanding about the comparable riskiness of certain investments does not play out in the market.

To further bring home the point about a stock's risk, consider the following example. When an after-hours earnings announcement hits the wire services saying that a stock's earnings are not in line with analysts' estimates, then the stock could easily drop 10% to 25%. Moreover, if the industry or sector that the stock resides in encounters some bad news during the day, all the stocks in that sector will probably drop in price.

Interestingly, most individual investors make their stock market decisions with their ears (listening to gurus and commentators) and stomachs instead of their brains. They hate to take losses on their investments because they think doing so reflects negatively on their intelligence. That is the main reason they buy a stock, for example, at $90 and ride it down to $10 before selling out in disgust at the lows. Buying high and selling low is not a successful investing formula. *The most important risk decision you need to make is the maximum acceptable loss that you will tolerate.* After you determine that loss figure, you should implement a stop-loss approach wherever possible, to minimize catastrophic losses.

For example, the investor buying the mentioned $90 stock should have used a stop-loss order of $81, assuming that the investor had a 10% maximum drawdown. This practice should be done routinely, and immediately after all new equity positions are established. Unfortunately, most investors do not take this step because that would be admitting to themselves that they could be wrong in their stock selection and lose some money. This can turn out to be a deadly decision, which can lead to financial ruin if there are too many losses over time. (Later in this chapter, you'll be able to consider stop-loss orders and how to use them.)

Another major flaw in investors' behavior is that they are always looking to "get back even" when a stock they bought declines in price, rather than saying to themselves, "Would I buy this stock today?" If the answer is no, they should consider selling the loser and deploying the funds in a more opportune investment. Some stocks, like the high-flying tech stocks bought at the 2000 peak, or the crushed blue-chips that got demolished in the latest bear market romp, will never get back to break-even.

If you find that you can't sleep at night because you are worried about your investments tanking, you should probably stay completely out of the stock market and place your money in high-quality corporate, government, and municipal bonds (or mutual funds or ETFs), CDs, or money market accounts. Keep in mind that the existing low interest rates on CDs and money market accounts, coupled with the federal income tax bite, will whittle down the gains on those vehicles to almost nothing. And you definitely won't keep up with inflation.

Avoiding the stock market entirely may require you to save more, reduce your expenses, and reduce your debt to support your current lifestyle. Inflation will eat into your returns from your fixed-income investments. That is why you and other investors buy equities—they grow faster than inflation over the long term. But if you do not feel comfortable owning individual stocks or stock mutual funds, stay away from them or invest a small portion of your funds in them. However, if you find that the investing approach explained in this book suits your needs and personality, you may find that you now have a plan of action that you are comfortable with (that can keep you on the right side of the market all the time), and that also allows you to have a peaceful night's sleep while growing your nest egg.

Diversification Risk

The second type of risk is diversification risk. Diversification's main tenet is that if you spread out your investment dollars among various non-correlated asset classes (for example, bonds, stocks—domestic and international—commodities, real estate, and cash), you will do well over time. Since Wall Street pundits proclaim that no one can predict the future, or know in advance which are the best classes to be invested in, they profess that investors need to spread their money among all classes. The point is that while some of your investments will fall in price during a market decline, others will hopefully rise. That is not a guarantee but a hope, which usually bears fruit. Unfortunately, the pundits don't mention the downside of diversification, which is that you'll be investing in some weak or underperforming market segments that will drive down your overall return.

One major point not mentioned by the Wall Street community is that there are always asset classes that are performing better than others over months or years at a time. And if you had invested and stayed with those investments or had a higher percentage of your portfolio in them, as opposed to other investment classes, you would have had a significantly better return on your money. For example, during 1995 through 1998, large-cap stocks outperformed small-cap stocks by a two-to-one margin. From 2004 to 2007, foreign stocks were the leading stock group. They beat bonds and large growth stocks by a wide margin. Every year there are asset classes that lead and lag.

In the ideal world, investors who diversify their portfolio using stocks and bonds (whether actual securities or mutual funds or ETFs) based on their predetermined risk tolerance should do well. Typically, a diversified portfolio will provide a higher return with less risk than a handful of securities or ones that are highly correlated with each other. Correlation refers to the relationship of one's portfolio or one's stock to another one. Two perfectly correlated portfolios would be said to have a correlation coefficient of 1.00. Alternatively, two perfectly uncorrelated portfolios would be said to have a correlation coefficient of –1.00.

For example, an actively managed large-cap growth mutual fund price performance would be measured against the S&P 500 benchmark. Comparing the two, the correlation coefficient is probably close to 1. Comparing this growth fund to a bond fund may yield a correlation coefficient of 0.25, indicating that they are only 25% related in their performance trend.

In bear markets, diversification only helps investors if they are invested with a high allocation to the best asset classes. During the crash of 2000-2002, bonds (based on the Barclays Capital U.S. Aggregate Index) averaged a *positive* 10.1% return per year, and small-cap value stocks went up in 2000 and 2001, 22.8% and 14.0% respectively, but finally succumbed in 2002 by dropping 11.4%. Even all S&P 500 sectors (such as energy, healthcare, financial, technology) were down in 2002 and 2008. Investors who joined the crowd and tried to make a "killing" by loading up on technology stocks in early 2000 lost 42%, 23%, and 39%, respectively, over those three years. Interestingly, the year after the 2002 bottom turned out to be a very positive stock market with a gain of 25%.

Diversification did not work out well in the 2008 stock market debacle. A typical diversified portfolio *lost 32%*. Only long-term bonds (+5.24%) and cash had positive returns. All nine S&P sector ETFs fell with an average sector loss of 35.55%. The same situation occurred in 2002 where the average sector loss was 18.41%. So, sometimes equity sector diversification does not provide any upside cushion.

Normally, value and international stocks and bonds provide defensive positive performance in bear markets, but not this time around. Only long-term treasury bonds had a positive return during this period. In 2008, international stocks dropped 43%, large-cap value stocks dropped 39.2%, and small-cap value stocks dropped 28.9%. Unfortunately, no one would have known this ahead of time. Amazingly, 2009 turned out to be a positive year, even after the debacle in the first quarter. Certainly, the phenomenal 60+% rally from the March 6, 2009, low was unexpected in such a short time frame, but welcomed by investors whose battered portfolios needed relief.

Diversifying into all asset classes results in having some weakly performing ones, and those act as a drag on your portfolio's performance. Wouldn't it be great to have a way to invest most of your money in just the asset classes that have the potential of beating the averages? As you will see in Chapter 3, you can accomplish that task by having an investing plan that focuses on selecting the top-performing components of each asset class.

Predetermined Portfolio Rebalancing Can Hurt Performance

Most financial advisors recommend that investors' portfolios be rebalanced at least annually, typically on January 1, or quarterly so that they retain their original asset class percentages within about 5 percentage points. If an asset class rises above this percentage, a portion will be sold to bring it back to the targeted level, and the proceeds placed in asset classes that have declined in value.

Unfortunately, rebalancing the portfolio on a particular fixed date makes no sense because certain asset classes may have long periods (for example, months or years) of continued outperformance compared to other asset classes held in the portfolio. Selling them arbitrarily on a fixed date because they went up more in relationship to the total portfolio and buying the other asset classes that have not done well is a backward way of investing.

The more intelligent approach is to invest in the right asset classes at the right time and switch to other asset classes as they start outperforming the current classes. This approach allows you to avoid the weakest asset classes that would reduce your overall performance. Without a specific strategy to determine the strength of asset classes, you have no way of knowing when to make these changes. That is why you should consider using a relative-strength approach in which each potential investment is compared to the others to see which ones are performing better over the past six months, for example.

Inflation Risk

The last type of risk an investor needs to be concerned about is inflation risk. Inflation withers away your buying power as the value of the dollar diminishes over time. According to the Bureau of Labor Statistics, a basket of goods worth $100 in 1970 cost $534.39 in 2007. Just consider that an entire pizza cost $1 in 1957 compared to $15 today. The only asset class to consistently outpace inflation over the long term has been stocks, but we don't know the stock market's future returns. Investing in stocks does not guarantee that you will outpace inflation, particularly when the market falls for decades at a time, as we have recently experienced. Bonds offer decent returns, but they may not exceed inflation. On a risk vs. return basis, you know that you need to be invested in stocks with a portion of your money so you can keep ahead of inflation and have enough capital in your old age to meet your needs. You also know that taxes eat into your returns as well, whether they be capital gains taxes on stocks not in retirement accounts or taxes on stock dividends, mutual fund distributions, and interest received on bonds (except for municipals).

Protecting Your Principal Is Paramount

Based on all the factors that enter the risk equation mentioned in this chapter, coupled with your own experience in the markets (if you've been investing), you should have a very good idea as to whether you are a conservative, moderate, or aggressive investor. After you've classified yourself, you can use this key piece of information to develop your action plan and choose your investment vehicles.

Use Stop Orders to Protect Profits and Minimize Losses

Now that you are aware of the riskiness of investing, it is important to understand the importance of taking steps to minimize losses on any investments before they mushroom out of control. One approach that has worked well for many investors is the use of stop orders.

You can place stop orders after you make your purchase of stocks or ETFs, or at any time thereafter. The purpose is to make sure that any potential loss does not become too large. Too many investors ride down a 5% or 10% stock loss to 50% or 75% because they can't stomach taking any loss because of ego or other emotional factors.

Most investors infrequently use stop orders. However, stop orders should be used to protect principal from major loss and to protect profits from turning into losses. Not using a stop order can be a big mistake and can be costly. Stops are there to prevent a financial disaster. And we've had two stock market meltdowns since 2000. Stop orders can be used for stocks and ETFs, but typically not for mutual funds, because they are priced at the close of business each trading day.

Determining Stop Price Is Not an Exact Science

You may be unfamiliar with stops and therefore unsure of where to place the stop-loss price—using a fixed percentage decline from the purchase price, using the average true range (ATR) method, using a price based on a support level as seen on a daily chart, using a break of a trend line, using a break of a moving average or other criteria. This subject alone would entail an entire chapter beyond the scope of this book's focus. Suffice it to say that whatever method you decide to use, it is better than not having any stops in place at all. No stop methodology will be perfect and a stock can quickly reverse up from where you were stopped out. That's life. That doesn't mean that you can't get back in and buy it back if it reverses direction. You will encounter price whipsaws and you may sell at the bottom of a trend channel; but there is nothing you can do about it. Just make the best decisions you can going forward, and don't waste your time looking back. As long as you gain knowledge and keep learning, you'll do fine.

Common Stop Orders

These are the common type of stop orders:

- **Limit order**—An order placed in a brokerage account to buy or sell a certain number of shares of a security at a specific price or better.
- **Stop-limit order**—The limit order is executed at the limit price or better when the stop price has been hit. It is a combination of a stop order and a limit order, which can be set at different prices.
- **Stop-loss order**—An order entered to sell at the next market price after the stop price has been attained.
- **Trailing stop order**—A stop-loss order that trails the price of the security at a specified percentage that changes as the security's price changes. For example, suppose you purchase a stock at $20 with a 10% trailing stop. Assume that the price rises to $25. The trailing stop will be set at $22.50, or 10% below the

existing price. The stop price doesn't change until the price rises above $25, and then a new trailing stop price is set. So at worst the investor will get $22.50 for the sale, unless the stock gaps down on the open and declines below $22.50. Then the investor will get the best available price at the time.

All these orders can be entered as Good Till Cancelled (GTC) or as a day order. For most investors, the GTC order is the one to use, because it stays open until it is executed, even if the investor is on vacation and not watching the market situation.

More on Using Trailing Stops to Protect Profits

Additionally, you should consider using trailing stops to protect profits on stocks and ETFs that are rising in price. Trailing stops are offered in most brokerage platforms and investors can easily set them up online. Some firms have advanced order choices, such as bracket stops and "OCO (one cancels the other)." Make sure that you contact your brokerage firm and check out their stop options.

You can set the stop at any percentage away from the current price that you desire. For example, you could set the trailing stop at 10%. That means that as the stock or ETF rises, the stop price will change accordingly. A $25 stock will have a stop price of $22.50 (10% from the current price), and if it rises to $35, the stop price automatically rises to $31.50.

Setting the amount of trailing stop is tricky. You could select an arbitrary percentage like 10% to 15%, or use the average true range[3] (ATR) or other methods, to come up with the stop amount. However, none of them will be perfect. And you may end up being whipsawed numerous times in a range-bound market.

In Figure 2.1 of QQQQs, you can see the ATR plotted as a separate indicator. During the high market volatility during September and October 2008, the daily ATR ranged between 1.25 and 2.25, whereas normally it hovers around 0.50 to 0.75.

Figure 2.1   PowerShares QQQQ with the Average True Range indicator

Source: Chart provided courtesy of Stockcharts.com

One argument against trailing stops is that normal market volatility might take you out of a position too early in the stock's advance if the trailing stop is set too tightly. That is true, but no one knows how far a stock will fall after it starts dropping. Also, you can buy back the stock again when it starts rising and the overall market is in an up trend.

Final Point

You need to determine your risk tolerance and make sure your investments mirror that level. It is also critical to manage your money and financial matters carefully, as life expectancies are increasing. Many individuals will live into their 80s and 90s. Social Security, savings, and pensions may not be sufficient to cover their needs. That's why people invest in the market—to grow their money for their retirement and to help pay for their children's or grandkids' education. If you want to be a successful investor, you need to use a systematic approach to managing and protecting your money. And, above all, you need to avoid bear markets that can damage your wealth and put you years behind in your plans to retire. Defense is critical in a bear market and that's why you need an action plan that incorporates a method to take you out of the market to protect your principal. Now that you understand the importance of determining your risk tolerance and protecting against market declines using stop orders, the next step is to incorporate your risk parameters into a detailed investment plan. That topic is covered in the next chapter.

Endnotes

1 Black, Pamela J. "Standard Risk Profile Questionnaires Don't Tell Advisors Enough About Their Clients' Appetite for Risk." *On Wall Street*, August 2009.

2 Levisohn, Ben. "Investor Stress Tests." *BusinessWeek*, August 10, 2009.

3 The average true range (ATR) was defined by J. Welles Wilder, in his book *New Concepts in Technical Trading Systems* (1978). The ATR is a moving average (usually 14 days) of the True Ranges. It is a measure of a stock's price movement. Many Internet sites and charting software programs provide this indicator. High ATR values indicate large intraday price changes, while low values indicate that prices are fairly stable. According to Investopedia.com, the True Range indicator is the greatest of the following:

The current high less the current low

The absolute value of the current high less the previous close

The absolute value of the current low less the previous close

3

Personal Investing Plan: Six-Step Road Map to Success

"There are two kinds of investors: those who don't know where the market is headed, and those who don't know that they don't know. Then again, there is a third type of investor—the investment professional, who indeed knows that he or she doesn't know, but whose livelihood depends upon appearing to know."

William Bernstein, *The Intelligent Asset Allocator*

"For those properly prepared in advance, a bear market in stocks is not a calamity but an opportunity."

John Templeton, investor, philanthropist, mutual fund pioneer, and billionaire

According to the Investment Company Institute, many investors heavily loaded up on mutual funds as the market was peaking in early 2000, and then heavily sold funds throughout the 2008 slide. Their behavior illustrates that too many investors are using emotion rather than logic to make their investment decisions. To become a better investor, you need a practical written investment plan that suits your individual needs, time frame, and risk tolerance. And you need to refer to it before making buy and sell decisions. Therefore, you should keep it prominently displayed. Your personal investment plan will become your road map to investing success.

Protecting your principal by avoiding bear markets is critical to your overall bottom-line results. This is difficult to accomplish unless you or your adviser (if you have one) pay attention to the market's tell-tale signs of trend change, and then take action to avoid the down-trend. That's why you need to incorporate specific "sell" criteria in the plan to take defensive action when the market is starting to slide. Just by crafting your own personal investing plan, you'll be way ahead of the vast majority of investors—since they rely on buy-and-hope, and that translates into having no plan at all.

If you want to trade with a portion of your money, as opposed to investing in the stock market, then you will need a separate "trading" plan that focuses on the short term. Unless you are positive that potentially losing that money will not impact you and your family financially, do not even consider a separate trading account. Keep your investing and trading plans and accounts separate or you'll get confused. What follows is an investing plan for your consideration that enables you to be in total control of your investments under all market conditions.

After many decades of investing in the stock market, I've concluded that buying-and-holding is risky and can lead to huge losses; therefore, I've developed a more realistic, easy-to-use approach that will help you become a more consistent and more profitable investor and provide you with the key to investment success which is to know *what to buy, when to buy, and when to sell*. Profits need to be taken every so often; otherwise, you may give them back over and over again in bear markets. That is not a smart way to manage your money. Therefore, I've provided you with a realistic, easy-to-implement, step-by-step investing plan that will help you become a more consistent and profitable investor.

Step 1: Determine Your Current Risk Level

Based on your understanding of risk presented in the preceding chapter and any further research you may have done on the subject, coupled with your actual investing experience, you should now have a clearer picture as to the type of investor you are—conservative, moderate, or aggressive. You can now determine the percentage of stocks (equity ETFs) vs. bonds (bond ETFs) you feel comfortable holding. You may decide that for your retirement accounts, you are an aggressive investor since you prefer a mix of 75% equities/25% bonds because of a 20-year or longer time horizon. On the other hand, in your nonretirement brokerage account you may prefer a mix of 50% stocks/50% bonds, putting you in the moderate camp. If you are in your 20s and 30s, and you classify yourself as a very aggressive investor, then you may decide to invest 100% in equities in your retirement account and 80% stocks/20% bonds in your regular brokerage account. The choice of your investment profile is up to you, and you don't have to conform to anyone else's opinion of what type of investing is best for you.

Step 2: Review Your Existing Investment Portfolios

Now that you have determined your risk tolerance, investor profile, and percent allocations to stocks vs. bonds, the next step is to gather all your brokerage accounts and retirement statements and open the latest statement for each account, if you haven't recently done so. During the market's precipitous drop in 2008 and early 2009, many investors were afraid to open their statements, because they didn't want to experience a stroke or heart attack. That was not a wise decision. It illustrates that they obviously were not using any defensive tactics to protect their capital before it was too late. Now that the market has recovered a large portion of the drop, it is time for you to look at all your investments and *plan ahead* so that you never again have to feel afraid to open your statements.

You'll want to analyze your existing portfolios to determine whether they reflect your current allocation preference. You may find that your existing investment allocations do not match your preferred allocations going forward. That is fine, since you can change each portfolio's look as you make changes going forward. Now at least you have a specific target allocation to strive for.

First, focus on your nonretirement account statements. Make a list of your investments using a spreadsheet program, the price you paid, the purchase date, the number of shares owned, the current price (use *The Wall Street Journal* or *Barron's* or go online to bigcharts.com or any related site to key in the ticker symbols to obtain the latest price), and your profit or loss on each position.

Next, follow the same approach for each retirement account, including IRAs, 401(k)s, 403(b)s, defined contribution plans, and the like. One suggestion is to put all your investments into separate portfolios available on any of the popular free financial Web sites. Another option is to use a spreadsheet to track each separate portfolio. Monitoring your positions on a weekly or at minimum a monthly schedule is suggested so that you know your total profit and loss situation at all times. There should not be any surprises.

Step 3: Assess the Stock Market's Condition

After reading Chapter 5, "The Stock Market Dashboard—Key Stock Market Indicators to Gauge the Market's Direction," you will be able to determine whether the stock market is in an uptrend, downtrend, or trading range, and whether the unique "Stock Market Dashboard" has triggered a "buy" or "sell" signal. The dashboard is composed of eight indicators that will alert you as to when to be in and out of the market. The dashboard range of readings goes from a low of –8 to a high of +8. A minimum reading of a +3 indicates an all-clear signal to make stock market purchases. This buy signal means that you should consider investing new money in our recommended list of ETFs (refer to Step 4). If the dashboard reaches a –3 reading or worse, you should consider liquidating all of your current positions and going into cash equivalents in all your accounts. After completing Chapter 5, you will have a complete understanding of how to use the dashboard as an early warning signal of impending market trend changes in both directions. You will then be able to avoid bear markets that will protect your capital and allow you to have better overall returns over time, as well as participate in bull markets at their take-off points.

Step 4: Invest in a Selected Universe of ETFs

As is explained in detail in the next chapter (Chapter 4, "Exchange-Traded Funds—The Most Suitable Investment Vehicles"), I have recommended specific exchange-traded funds (ETFs) be used as your investment vehicle of choice instead of stocks, bonds, and mutual funds. ETFs are liquid, inexpensive, transparent, and available in many asset categories, and can be bought and sold during the day. After providing information on the ETF basics, I've included a specific ETF investing universe of 66 of the 744 available ETFs to be used in your investing plan. Specifically, you should consider investing in the top-performing ETFs from the following five diverse asset categories:

1. Morningstar Style Box (for example, value or growth; small-, mid-, and large-cap)
2. S&P Market Sectors (for example, energy, healthcare, and technology)
3. International—countries (for example, Brazil, Canada, Israel, Australia, and Malaysia)

4. Fixed Income (for example, corporate, treasury and municipal bonds)

5. Specialty (for example, gold, silver, oil, and agriculture)

Going forward, ETFs should be used to replace any stocks or
mutual funds sold in your existing portfolios, wherever possible.
Obviously, in certain retirement accounts you will not have any ETF
options, as the number and selection of investments is restricted by
your workplace's plan offerings. But in your self-directed IRA
accounts, SEPs, and nonretirement accounts, you can buy and sell
ETFs, as your investment vehicle of choice, using a discount brokerage account totally under your control.

Step 5: Select Top-Ranked ETFs Based on Relative Strength Analysis

As you know, diversification among asset classes is a cornerstone
of investing. However, the way to maximize diversification is to invest
in the best-performing ETFs in each of the five asset classes. Relative
strength analysis compares one ETF's price performance to that of
the others in its asset category, or in a particular universe of ETFs. I
have selected a six-month time frame for price performance to rank
the ETFs in each asset class to find the leaders.

Numerous studies have shown that this time frame works well for
assessing future price performance. The rationale is that the strongest
ETFs will stay strong for weeks or months at a time and outperform
the lower-ranking ETFs. When the top-ranked ETFs begin to falter to
a preset level, you should replace them with the stronger ones. When
you read Chapter 6, "Using Relative Strength Analysis to Determine
Where to Invest," you will see how simple it is to find the cream of the
crop. Also, you will be provided with two free Internet Web sites to
obtain the top-performing ETFs. Be sure to review the details and
components of each ETF before you invest because you need to know
exactly what you are investing in. You can use the ETF family Web sites
provided in Chapter 6, as well as www.morningstar.com (ETF tab).

When investing cash, you should be sure to spread your funds among the top ETFs in each of the five major categories, according to your risk tolerance and your ratio of equity to bond ETFs. Chapter 4 on ETFs provides the number of ETFs to purchase in each category. If you are a conservative or moderate investor, that is the approach you should consider. If you are a more aggressive investor, you may want to consider investing only in the top-ranked ETFs from the combined 66 ETF universe, instead of selecting a few from each of the five asset classes. However, that approach entails a higher degree of risk because you may have a concentration of ETFs that are not at all diversified according to your risk profile.

The decision to pick the top ETFs irrespective of asset class may result in your being 100% invested in equity ETFs. On occasion, there is the possibly that 90% or more of those ETFs will be the international countries, which are much more volatile than the other ETF categories. You will be able to gain further insight into this scenario by reviewing the ETF relative strength data tables presented in Chapter 6. In fact, international ETFs were the top performers of all the asset classes in late 2009.

Step 6: Protect Your Portfolio Using Stops

Even with the careful and methodical investing approach presented in this book, you need to understand that investment profits are never guaranteed. Therefore, you should always consider placing a stop-loss order immediately after you make an ETF purchase. Refer to the preceding chapter to review the various stop-loss order choices. Moreover, be sure to use trailing stops when a position starts making money. Alternatively, instead of using stops, you could buy put options on the major indices or buy a specific dollar amount of an inverse ETF (rises in price when the market declines). However, those choices cost money and will decay rapidly in price if the market continues to rise. Always consider defensive tactics when making ETF purchases since the future is unpredictable. All you can do is put the odds in your favor, watch your portfolio very carefully, and take action when necessary. At times your stop orders will trigger before the dashboard signals a change in market direction. At that point, you'll have to determine the most appropriate course of action. It's always better to lock in a sure profit or minimize an existing loss than to risk a more difficult situation going forward.

Investing for Retirement

I have included this section on retirement investing because it requires a different mind-set, as well as an adjustment to your investing plan compared to investing in nonretirement accounts. Investing for retirement should be a major component of your overall financial plan. Depending on your age and the number of years before you retire, you can set up a plan of action to meet your goals. In 2007 in the United States, individuals legally gambled with $92.3 billion of their money, while saving only $57.4 billion.[1] This backward relationship on priorities works against those who need to save the most for retirement and other needs.

U.S. retirement assets were $14 trillion at year-end 2008, which decreased by $3.9 trillion or 22% from the prior year. There were 47.3 million households with an IRA account with 90% invested in traditional IRAs. Approximately 65% of the funds invested in retirement accounts were placed in equity mutual funds.[2] According to an Edward Jones survey of adults over age 18 conducted by Opinion Research and published in the *USA Today*,[3] 32% of the respondents indicated that it would take two to five years to reclaim their retirement account losses. Almost 25% said it would take at least six years, and 10% said they would never recover their losses.

The Bear Market Impact Is Devastating

The bear market that dominated 2008 ravaged retirement accounts, especially for those with an aggressive risk tolerance—

having 75% or more of their money invested in the equity markets. It could be a few years or more for those workers to get back to even to their account value on October 9, 2007, the last market peak. Moreover, just about 40% of employers have stopped or reduced their matching contributions. Unfortunately, most workers did not save as much as possible when building their retirement account; therefore, they may face financial difficulties during their retirement years. Unbelievably, about 50% of for-profit company workers between 25 and 65 had no employer retirement plan.

Retirement Accounts Offer Tax Advantages and Compounding of Principal

Due to the tax advantages available for retirement accounts and the opportunity for tax-free compounding of returns over a lifetime, young investors, in general, should try to maximize their annual contributions (especially if their employer provides a match in their 401(k) plans) and consider investing aggressively for the majority of the years and more conservatively within five years of retirement. Obviously, as an investor you need to assess your ability to fund the account each year, the amount to fund, the estimated time horizon before withdrawals are expected, your risk tolerance level to feel comfortable, and your other financial priorities and obligations. Everyone will have different time frames, goals, and funding capability.

Retirement accounts include the overwhelmingly popular traditional IRA, the ever-growing Roth IRA, the SEP for the self-employed and small businesses, the 401(k) for individuals at many companies, and the 403(b) for government, hospital, and school district employees, among others. Some workers are fortunate enough to have defined benefit plans funded by their employers, but these types of plans are now in the minority. The major benefit of retirement accounts is the tax-free compounding of assets over many years and the continued tax deduction of the invested amounts. The Roth IRA is a different animal, because after-tax money is used for the purchase and there is no initial tax deduction, but when this IRA is cashed in after age 59 1/2, there is no Federal tax due on any of it.

In all cases, except the Roth IRA, the account owner will owe tax only after the funds are withdrawn from the account. They will pay income tax at their existing tax rate. Most individuals take their distributions after age 59 1/2 (to avoid the 10% Federal Tax surcharge on early withdrawal). In the year after age 70 1/2, the owner must take Required Minimum Distributions (RMDs) or face a steep IRS penalty. There is an option to withdraw retirement funds after age 55 in equal installments known as the 72(t) payments. Investors need to check with their financial advisors and accountants for details on how this approach works and the specific requirements so that they don't make any egregious costly mistakes, one of which is being charged the 10% early-withdrawal penalty.

Investment Choices Vary by Plan

In most of the at-work retirement plans, the individual can invest in a fixed group of investments, usually mutual funds from a few families. And in some cases fixed and variable annuities are offered. Self-employed persons, in their retirement plans, have a wider choice and can also purchase individual stocks, bonds, annuities, ETFs, and other vehicles. When you leave your job, you can roll over your 401(k) or 403(b) into a traditional IRA and then invest in a wider range of vehicles than is offered by most employers. Some individuals leave their existing retirement accounts with their previous employer for any number of reasons, but usually more investment choices are available with a rollover IRA opened as a brokerage account, mutual fund family, and so forth.

More and more employers are moving toward low-cost index funds and ETFs in their 401(k) offerings to employees. Currently, about 90% of the $1.5 trillion invested in these plans and other defined benefit plans is invested in actively managed mutual funds. In a survey of 150 employers, 17% were planning to switch from their actively managed mutual funds to index funds. That was double the number of firms from 2007. One 401(k) record-keeping firm has received more than 100 employer inquiries about adding ETFs to their plans after the firm added them to their platform as an option.[4]

The time frame for most retirement accounts exceeds 20 years, and can run as long as 50 years, depending on when the individual begins working and contributing. The opportunity to amass a substantial nest egg is enticing. Since the invested money and the dividends and capital appreciation are compounded over time, the final totals can be astonishing. Investors can be more aggressive in their retirement accounts if they have at least a 10-year and preferably a 20-year or longer time horizon, because the longer the time frame, the better the odds for positive returns. But they still need to be defensive investors so that their portfolios do not get clobbered again. As seen in the past decade, two bear markets have resulted in investors not making any progress in their accounts since 1998. This is quite different from the total return performance of the S&P 500 index in the 1980s and 1990s, during which the average annual return was 17.55% and 18.20%, respectively.

No Capital Losses Are Available in Retirement Accounts

Keep in mind that if your retirement investments lose money, you cannot take any capital losses on your tax return. For example, assume you purchased five mutual funds in 1996 in your traditional IRA for a total of $5,000 and invested another $45,000 over the years. Assume that you cashed them in year-end 2008 when they were worth $62,000 in total and you were age 63. You would be taxed on $62,000 at your existing tax rate. Let's assume that of the five funds, one had a loss of $7,000 over the years. That loss is not tax-deductible because you pay tax on the value of the funds when you sell them.

Of course, in nonretirement accounts you are permitted to deduct $3,000 in capital losses a year, and carry forward additional losses to future years until they are used up. There are really no restrictions on where to invest. For example, a margin account can be opened and you can sell short. A retirement account does not permit this approach. You can invest in stocks, bonds, mutual funds, ETFs, and options. Retirement investor choices are much more restricted, as you have seen.

Retirement Investing Using Our Action Plan

Most likely you have one or more retirement accounts—some at work and some self-directed. Since you know that bear markets follow bull markets, and vice versa, it is critical for you to protect your account from losing value during bear market cycles. You can use the Stock Market Dashboard to ascertain when a "sell" signal is triggered, and then take defensive action by selling all positions and going into cash equivalents or bond funds. The key to building a large account balance when you retire is to preserve your principal during the bear markets, and then redeploy the funds into the top-ranked ETFs at the beginning of the bull market, based on a dashboard "buy" signal. You can accomplish both goals by following the six-step strategy put forth in this chapter.

You should consider being as aggressive as possible in your retirement accounts, especially if you have at least a 20-year time horizon. This long time frame will allow you to grow your account value into a hefty nest egg. Hopefully, if you use the strategy recommended you will be able to make money in all market conditions and be able to really compound your returns.

Endnotes

1 Zweig, Jason. "Using the Lottery Effect to Make People Save." *The Wall Street Journal*, July 18, 2009, p. B1.

2 ICI Research Fundamentals, June 2009, vol. 18 no. 5.

3 July 22, 2009, issue.

4 Laise, Eleanor. "More Index Fund Sought for 401(k)s." *The Wall Street Journal*, July 18, 2009, p. B1.

4

Exchange-Traded Funds—The Most Suitable Investment Vehicles

"The deeper one delves, the worse things look for actively managed funds."

William Bernstein, *The Intelligent Asset Allocator*

"Exchange-traded funds probably rank as the most successful financial product of the past two decades."

Edwin A. Finn Jr., *Barron's*, October 19, 2009

Now that we've covered the key elements necessary to invest successfully—namely understanding risk and using an investing plan—let's focus on *where to invest your money*. Believe it or not, that's where most investors go wrong. According to the findings of numerous behavioral finance studies, most investors' stock market performance is worse than the market averages, and their mutual fund investment performance suffers from poor timing due to emotional decision making—buying high and selling low. Most investors believe that they are more intelligent than other investors and that they can pick winning stocks most of the time. Actually both beliefs are false.

Amazingly, the typical investor's mutual fund performance has been consistently below that of the fund's actual performance. According to a March 9, 2009, press release from DALBAR, Inc., their research indicated that for the 20-year period ending in 2008, the average investor earned a 1.87% average annual in stock mutual funds compared to the S&P 500's return of 8.35% and the inflation rate of 2.89% per annum. Equity investors lost 41.6% in 2008 compared to a drop in the S&P 500 Index of 37.7%. Also, investors only held their funds for an average of 3.11 years in 2008, the shortest holding period since 2002.

Most investors have neither the proper psychological makeup nor the financial/forensic accounting expertise to be successful individual stock pickers. Even the majority of professional portfolio managers, certified financial analysts, investment advisors, and hedge fund managers who make big bucks have difficulty selecting stocks that beat the market on a consistent basis, especially in bear markets. Of course, there are exceptions, but they are few in number compared to the number playing the stock market game.

Investing in Actively Managed Mutual Funds Is Not Recommended

In 1980, 4.6 million households owned mutual funds for their regular investment and retirement plans, compared to 52.5 million at year-end 2008 (representing 45% of all U.S. households), according to the Investment Company Institute. As of year-end 2008, there were 8,889 mutual funds in existence with a total value of $9.6 trillion. Certainly, over the past 50 years mutual funds have been a viable alternative to individual stocks, since they offer diversification, reasonable risk parameters, low cost, and professional money management.

Majority of Active Fund Managers Have a Poor Track Record

The well-known and long-time Legg Mason Value Trust fund manager Bill Miller had a 15-year run of beating its S&P 500 benchmark until 2005. However, even his fund's performance has been underwhelming for the past 4 years running, culminating in 2008, when his fund got sheared by 55%. In 2009, though, he recovered and his fund jumped 29% in the second quarter, and 14% for the year through the end of June 2009 compared to 3.2% for the S&P year-to-date.

A Standard & Poor's 2008 study revealed that from 2003 through 2008, 70% of large-cap fund managers failed to match their benchmark. Moreover, this trend was also prevalent in all other funds categories, whether stocks, bonds, or emerging market funds.[1] A study titled "Luck Versus Skill in the Cross Section of Mutual Fund Returns," conducted by Professors Eugene Fama (University of Chicago Booth School of Business) and Kenneth French (Dartmouth), found that it was hard to determine if actively managed mutual funds beat their benchmark based on skill or luck. The professors believe that this study, which reviewed the performance of 3,156 equity mutual funds from January 1984 through September 2006, confirms their view that the majority of active managers can't beat their benchmarks on a consistent basis.[2] Their study found that, except for the best 3% of all funds, active managers' results were less than what would be delivered by pure chance.

Some mutual fund managers are now turning to market timing to enhance their performance. They are trying to sidestep big losses by using "tactical asset allocation" and going to big cash positions at opportune times, betting that they can minimize their losses in bear markets. For example, a new fund, Quaker Small-Cap Tactical Allocation Fund, had 50% of its assets in cash compared to 95% in 2008. John Hancock Technical Opportunities Fund was 90% in cash in early 2009. Other funds that can hold big cash positions include Encompass, Intrepid Small Cap, Ivy Asset Strategy, Van Kampen Global Tactical Asset Allocation, and Legg Mason Permal Tactical Allocation Fund.[3]

Since 2000 the mutual fund industry has launched 3,135 funds and closed or merged 2,971 funds for poor performance, falling asset base, or other reasons. Just in 2008 and 2009 (through September), the number of liquidations reached 438 and 423, respectively. There are still more than 8,000 mutual funds in existence, as there were a decade ago. Interestingly, as of September 30, 2009, there were 304 funds with only a one- or two-star Morningstar rating for the past three years.[4]

Index Funds Have Garnered Most of New Equity Mutual Fund Money

Over the past few years, the majority of investors have been funneling most of their mutual purchases directly into index funds, rather than the highly promoted actively managed funds. This trend indicates that investors are getting smarter as they realize that the poor track record of active managers versus their benchmarks is costing them money. Approximately 75% of active managers do not beat their benchmark over a ten-year time horizon, so paying higher internal operating expenses of greater than 1% for these active funds produces no value and reduces an investor's overall return.

Index funds are composed of stocks mirroring a specific index. The first index fund was the Vanguard 500 Index (based on the S&P 500 Index developed and offered by John Bogle at Vanguard). Its current assets total $77.8 billion. Other large well-known index funds include Fidelity Spartan Market Index ($10.3B), Vanguard Total Stock Market ($27B), Vanguard Small Cap Index ($5.4B), and Schwab 1000 ($4.3B). There are more than 300 index mutual funds in 24 categories. The weightings of indices vary. For example, market-capitalization weighted (S&P 500), price weighted (Dow Jones Industrial Avg.), and equally weighted (Value Line Composite Index) are the three main weightings used. A typical index fund has 100% of the funds invested in stocks that mimic the index, and the cash holdings are minimal. There is minimal portfolio turnover, and the securities are infrequently changed. Each index has a beta = 1.0 (a measure of volatility). Over long periods, the index usually beats the majority of active managers in its category, but usually in bear markets more active managers beat the index, but not by much.

No-load index funds are certainly a viable investment option for investors, but some fund families may charge redemption fees when the funds are sold. Moreover, ETFs are basically index funds and come in a wide selection of choices, so there is no major reason not to use them.

ETFs Are the Preferred Investment Vehicle

In 1993, the first ETF index portfolio, called the SPDRs, was offered to investors. Its full name was the Standard & Poor's Depositary Receipts (500 Stock Index), with ticker symbol SPY. As of August 30, 2009, its total assets were about $69.4 billion. ETF choices have mushroomed since then, reaching more than 100 in 2001 and totaling 744 by year-end 2008, valued at $531 billion. As of September 30, 2009, there were 768 ETFs valued at $695 billion. Since 1999, ETF assets have grown at an annual rate of 36%.[5] There are also hundreds of ETFs still in the registration process. This has resulted in the decline in ownership of active mutual funds compared to index mutual funds and ETFs. Even with the fast growth of ETFs over the past ten years, they only represent between 5–6% of traditional mutual fund assets.

Comparison of ETFs to Mutual Funds

Of all the approximately 768 ETFs, only 15 are using active management strategies that try to beat their comparable benchmark, while the remainder are passively managed—similar to index mutual funds. These 15 are scattered among the PowerShares and WisdomTree families.[6]

In simple terms, an all-equity ETF is a basket of stocks that mimics an index, such as the S&P 500, Dow Jones Industrials, or NASDAQ 100. The components are static and most ETFs are passively managed, thus the comparison to an index fund. Of course, there are other specialized ETFs that contain bonds, currencies, commodities, industries, sectors, and countries. Let's compare equity ETFs to mutual funds:

- Mutual funds are priced once at the end of the trading day. ETFs can be bought and sold throughout the day like stocks. ETFs can be considered a hybrid investment—a cross between a mutual fund and a stock.

- Individuals purchasing mutual funds can buy them through stockbrokers and financial advisors if they need advice and are not very knowledgeable. This will result in their paying an upfront load if they purchase an "A" share (a one-time fee usually ranging between 4.25% and 5.75% of the purchase price for an investment under $250,000) or paying a possible contingent deferred sales charge with a "C" share class (a 1% fee for selling the fund in the first year only and no upfront fee or redemption fee after one year). Another choice for an investor is to open a managed money account that invests in mutual funds in which the *annual management fee* depends on the assets under management. The starting fee for an investment of $50,000 to $100,000, for example, can range between 1% and 1.5%, depending on the firm. In this scenario either the advisor or the firm's portfolio managers usually actively manage the account. Investors who prefer to avoid these loads and fees can also buy mutual funds directly from a mutual fund family, if they offer no-load funds or through the many brokerage firms that offer a supermarket of mutual funds.

  Self-directed investors can buy ETFs by opening a brokerage account in which they pay a commission for each trade. Most investors select a discount brokerage firm that offers low commissions in the range of $1 to $10 per trade. A list of brokerage firms for your use is provided in Appendix 4.1. The typical commission is shown in this table, but check for deals based on opening a new account and having a minimum account balance to get better pricing. More information on discount brokers can be found here:

www.thedigeratilife.com/blog/index.php/2009/05/22/online-discount-brokers-smart-money-broker-survey

- Domestic stock mutual funds have higher overall annual expense ratios (averaging about 1.29% according to *Morningstar Mutual Funds,* October 24, 2009, edition), 12(b)-1 marketing fees, and a built-in cost for portfolio turnover (averaging 97% a year), which are reflected in the fund's closing price (known as net asset value) that day. These expenses can total at least 2% annually. On the other hand, ETFs have much lower annual expense ratios, averaging about 0.10% to 0.35% per fund, with some specialty funds being higher (0.50% to 0.95%). There are no ETF 12(b)-1 fees and the portfolio turnover is minimal, if any. Bond ETFs have an annual expense ratio of 0.24% compared to 0.91% for general bond mutual funds, according to Morningstar.

- Mutual funds are actively managed (except for index funds, which are passively managed), compared to the vast majority of ETFs that are passively managed. Thus, mutual funds have higher overall fees that are passed along to their investors. That is one reason most investors have been buying index mutual funds (instead of actively managed funds) that have the lowest mutual fund fees. For example, Schwab S&P 500 Fund's annual expense ratio is 0.09%, even lower than the popular Vanguard's Total Stock Market fund (0.16%). Some index mutual funds have lower fees than some comparable S&P 500 ETFs, so shop around before you invest.

- Stock mutual funds are almost fully invested during bear markets (most funds maintain about 5% to 7% in cash for redemptions). Mutual fund portfolio managers are mandated to be fully invested most of the time, as specified in their prospectus. Even if those managers want to build up cash reserves because they know they are in a new or continuing bear market, they are restricted from doing so. That is the main problem with owning stock mutual funds in bear markets. One issue is that if the fund fails to be fully invested and the market rises, their cash position will act as a drag on the fund's performance and result in performance below the category benchmark. That's a problem for a fund manager since at worst he wants to equal the benchmark, not underperform it. On the other hand, self-directed investors can buy a ProFunds or Rydex inverse mutual fund that rises when the market drops, thus making money as the market drops. The other choice is to buy inverse ETFs, which are also offered by the same two firms.

A few mutual funds, such as Stadion Managed Fund, FPA Income, and Third Avenue Value, are able to hold large cash positions if they feel that this is the best strategy. That is what they did in the 2008–2009 bear market, but even so they still took negative hits in their performance. On the other hand, investors do not have to remain invested in stocks or ETFs during bear markets. They can sell them, buy put options, sell call options, or buy inverse ETFs that rise as the market falls. Inverse ETFs are covered later in this chapter.

• Most stock mutual funds declare capital gains distributions at year-end during profitable years, and these distributions can be substantial. Even though the mutual fund investors did not sell the fund during the year, they have to pay capital gains tax on this distribution (if not a retirement account) when they file their tax returns. They can adjust their cost basis to reflect this distribution so that when the fund is sold the correct tax calculation is made. Some investors can sell their mutual fund before the record date to avoid the distribution. Most ETFs (except for the leveraged ones) pay zero or minimal capital gain distributions, and the investor can always sell the ETF before the distribution's record date.

• Stock and bond mutual funds tend to have more frequent portfolio turnover than similarly structured ETFs because they are actively managed. Therefore, the mutual fund expenses are higher and are passed along to the clients.

Exchange-Traded Fund (ETF) Basics

ETFs are baskets of securities, bonds, currencies, commodities, or other components depending on the index, sector, or industry that they are replicating. They are basically mutual fund substitutes that mimic an index fund. One unique ETF feature is that they trade all day long. Therefore, investors have the option of timing their purchase during the day to suit their needs. This option is particularly useful in volatile markets where the DJIA can move in 200- to 500-point ranges in a day. In September 2008, the DJIA lost 777 points in one day, not a very good day for investors holding ETFs, but a great day for those holding inverse ETFs. The heaviest users of ETFs are institutions, professional traders, and investment advisors. Currently, ETFs account for about 40% of the stock market volume.[7] And bond ETFs account for about 15% of all the industry assets.

ETF Families

More than a dozen ETF families offer a wide variety of ETFs in all categories. Table 4.1 provides a listing of the major families and their Web sites for further information. A number of these Web sites have a significant amount of information on their funds' composition, performance, and other key characteristics, as well as ETF education and some templates. Before investing in any ETF, be sure to check it out on the family site as well as www.morningstar.com, which contains detailed information on all ETFs.

Investment Categories

ETFs are available in a wide range of investment categories:

- *Capitalization* (large-cap, mid-cap, small-cap, and micro-cap). In general, a definition of capitalization is as follows: Large-cap, top 5% in market with cap greater than $10 billion; mid-cap, next 15% of companies; small-cap, remainder (less than $1.4 billion); micro-cap, less than $500 million.
- *Style* (value, growth, and core [a combination of the two] used in the preceding cap categories).
- *Broad stock market* (total stock market, S&P 500, NASDAQ, Dow Jones Industrials, Russell 2000, and many more).
- *Sectors* (for example, the Select Sector SPDRS, including healthcare, financial, utilities, energy, technology, consumer discretionary, materials, and industrial). Note: There are ten S&P sectors, but only nine sector ETFs.

TABLE 4.1   A Sampling of ETF Families

Name of Family	Web Site Address	Number of ETFs	Type of ETFs
iShares (now under BlackRock name)	http://us.ishares.com	187	Wide variety including international (84), commodities, real estate, and specialty
State Street Global Advisors	www.spdrs.com	88	Wide variety including fixed income and equities
Vanguard	www.vanguard.com	39	Wide variety
ProShares	www.proshares.com	90	Leveraged bull, bear, and sector style, international and fixed income
PowerShares	www.invescopowershares.com	116	Wide variety+ 5 actively managed
Market Vectors	www.vaneck.com	21	Hard assets, international, specialty, and munibond
Direxion	www.direxionshares.com/etfs	22	Leveraged bull and bear—up to 3 times
WisdomTree	www.wisdomtree.com	51	Wide variety plus earnings and dividend focused
Rydex/SGI	www.rydex-sgi.com	40	Leveraged bull and bear plus nine currency shares
Claymore	www.claymore.com/etf	34	Variety
First Trust	www.ftportfolios.com	39	Sector, style, specialty, and international
Pimco	www.pimcoetfs.com	5	Fixed income—treasury and TIPs

- *Industries* (for example, real estate, construction, brokers and asset managers, shipping, timber, Internet, global wind, water, insurance, aerospace, biotechnology, and telecommunications, among others).
- *Fixed Income* (for example, U.S. Treasury bonds and T-bills, municipals, TIPS, preferred stock, corporate, high yield).
- *Global and International Stocks* (countries and regions—emerging markets, gulf states, Asia, Africa, and Middle East).
- *Commodities* (for example, gold, silver, metals, grains, biofuels, oil, agriculture, energy, natural gas, sugar, and tin, among others).
- *Currencies* (for example, U.S. Dollar, Euro, Australian Dollar, British Pound, Japanese Yen, Canadian Dollar, and Swiss Franc, among others).
- *Inverse* (ProShares, Rydex, and Direxion families), offering the ability to make money when the market drops.
- *Leveraged Long* (ProShares, Rydex, and Direxion families), offering double and triple beta funds (Direxion only) on stocks, fixed income, countries, and commodities. Each family has different offerings.
- *Leveraged Short* (ProShares, Rydex, and Direxion families), double and triple beta funds (Direxion only) on selected stocks, fixed income, countries, and commodities. Each family has different offerings.

Largest ETFs by Market Cap and Net Assets

Table 4.2 lists the 25 largest ETFs, based on market capitalization. Market cap is equal to the share price multiplied by the shares outstanding. Table 4.3 shows the largest individual ETFs by net assets. The ten top funds hold almost 40% of all the ETF assets.

TABLE 4.2   The 25 Largest ETFs by Market Cap

Symbol	Name	Market Cap°	Avg. Volume
SPY	SPDR S&P 500	$54,102.42	226,758,000
EFA	iShares MSCI EAFE Index Fund	$33,049.42	21,872,100
EEM	iShares MSCI Emerging Index Fund	$32,966.60	71,537,000
IVV	iShares S&P 500 Index Fund	$19,803.77	4,352,050
GLD	SPDR Gold Trust	$18,729.65	12,700,500
QQQQ	PowerShares QQQ Trust	$16,525.74	111,229,000
TIP	iShares Lehman TIPS Bond Fund	$16,477.49	1,156,710
LQD	iShares GS $ InvesTopTM Corporate Bond Fund	$13,566.76	1,153,430
VWO	Vanguard Emerging Markets ETF	$13,160.03	6,234,720
IWM	iShares Russell 2000	$12,046.60	52,566,900
AGG	iShares Lehman Aggregate	$10,660.78	625,542
IWF	iShares Russell 1000 Growth	$10,163.24	3,521,880
EWZ	iShares MSCI Brazil Index Fund	$10,105.09	17,926,300
FXI	iShares FTSE/Xinhua China 25 Index Fund	$8,771.22	24,807,400
IWD	iShares Russell 1000 Value	$8,068.81	2,579,250

TABLE 4.2 The 25 Largest ETFs by Market Cap (continued)

Symbol	Name	Market Cap°	Avg. Volume
MDY	SPDR MidCap Trust Series I	$7,524.09	4,753,540
SHY	iShares Barclays 1-3 Year Treasury	$7,318.14	908,186
DIA	Diamonds	$6,365.96	14,992,500
IJH	iShares S&P MidCap 400 Index Fund	$5,850.31	1,132,820
BND	Vanguard Total Bond Market ETF	$5,468.59	517,412
IVW	iShares S&P 500 Growth Index Fund	$5,350.02	1,429,620
EWJ	iShares MSCI Japan Index Fund	$5,064.89	28,534,600
DVY	iShares Dow Jones Select Dividend Index Fund	$4,838.47	522,316
IWB	iShares Russell 1000	$4,728.90	3,288,840
IJR	iShares S&P SmallCap 600 Index Fund	$4,723.47	1,699,200

Market Cap is shown in millions of dollars. Source: ETF Database

TABLE 4.3 Individual ETFs by Net Assets

Fund Name	Ticker	Category	Fund Family	Net Assets	Expense Ratio	Annual Turnover Ratio	Legal Type	Inception Date
SPDRs	SPY	Large Blend	SPDR Trust Series 1	$69.44B	0.09%	4.56%	FE	29-Jan-93
SPDR Gold Shares	GLD	N/A	streetTRACKS Gold Trust	$32.38B	0.40%	0.00%	FE	18-Nov-04
iShares MSCI EAFE Index	EFA	Foreign Large Blend	iShares Trust	$32.05B	0.34%	12.00%	FE	14-Aug-01
iShares MSCI Emerging Markets Index	EEM	Diversified Emerging Mkts	iShares Trust	$31.70B	0.72%	11.00%	FE	7-Apr-03
iShares S&P 500 Index	IVV	Large Blend	iShares Trust	$18.15B	0.09%	7.00%	FE	15-May-00
PowerShares QQQ	QQQQ	Large Growth	PowerShares QQQ Trust, Series 1	$16.19B	0.20%	10.00%	FE	10-Mar-99
iShares Barclays TIPS Bond	TIP	N/A	iShares Trust	$14.72B	0.20%	10.00%	FE	4-Dec-03
iShares iBoxx $ Invest Grade Corp Bond	LQD	Long-Term Bond	iShares Trust	$12.75B	0.15%	48.00%	FE	22-Jul-02

TABLE 4.3 Individual ETFs by Net Assets (continued)

Fund Name	Ticker	Category	Fund Family	Net Assets	Expense Ratio	Annual Turnover Ratio	Legal Type	Inception Date
Vanguard Emerging Markets Stock ETF	VWO	Diversified Emerging Mkts	Vanguard International Equity Index Fund	$11.40B	0.20%	20.00%	FE	4-Mar-05
Vanguard Total Stock Market ETF	VTI	Large Blend	Vanguard Index Funds	$11.34B	0.07%	5.00%	FE	24-May-01
iShares FTSE/Xinhua China 25 Index	FXI	Pacific/Asia ex-Japan Stk	iShares Trust	$11.30B	0.74%	24.00%	FE	5-Oct-04
iShares Russell 2000 Index	IWM	Small Blend	iShares Trust	$10.68B	0.20%	21.00%	FE	22-May-00
iShares Russell 1000 Growth Index	IWF	Large Growth	iShares Trust	$10.22B	0.20%	22.00%	FE	22-May-00
iShares Barclays Aggregate Bond	AGG	Intermediate-Term Bond	iShares Trust	$10.08B	0.20%	519.00%	FE	22-Sep-03
iShares MSCI Brazil Index	EWZ	Latin America Stock	iShares, Inc.	$8.86B	0.63%	30.00%	FE	10-Jul-00
iShares Russell 1000 Value Index	IWD	Large Value	iShares Trust	$7.55B	0.20%	22.00%	FE	22-May-00
DIAMONDS Trust, Series 1	DIA	Large Value	DIAMONDS Trust Series I	$7.31B	0.17%	11.27%	FE	13-Jan-98

TABLE 4.3 Individual ETFs by Net Assets (continued)

Fund Name	Ticker	Category	Fund Family	Net Assets	Expense Ratio	Annual Turnover Ratio	Legal Type	Inception Date
MidCap SPDRs	MDY	Mid-Cap Blend	MIDCAP SPDR TRUST SERIES 1	$7.21B	0.25%	28.95%	FE	27-Apr-95
iShares Barclays 1-3 Year Treasury Bond	SHY	Short Government	iShares Trust	$7.13B	0.15%	37.00%	FE	22-Jul-02
Financial Select Sector SPDR	XLF	Specialty-Financial	Select Sector SPDR Trust	$6.57B	0.22%	18.00%	FE	16-Dec-98

° All non-intraday data as of 31-Aug-09

Printed with permission of www.etfzone.com

ETF Benefits Are Extensive

ETFs offer investors significant benefits. Thus, they have become the investment vehicle of choice not only by smart investors, but also by many financial advisors, and some 401(k) providers. These benefits include the following:

- **Transparency**—The portfolio and percent invested in each position are accessible for all to see. Since most ETFs are index funds, the portfolio rarely changes. However, if the index that the ETF is mirroring changes, the ETF will make a change as well.
- **Liquidity**—ETFs can be sold throughout the trading day as a market, limit, or stop order.
- **Low expense ratio**—Annual expense ratios ranging from 0.1% to 0.35%, but higher for specialty and country funds (0.50% to 0.95%), but usually much lower than mutual funds.
- **No 12b-1 fees**—ETFs do not usually charge these marketing fees, but if they do there is a limit of 0.07%.
- **Tax-efficiency**—Minimal transactions or portfolio turnover, and therefore minimal capital gains distributions.
- **Passive management**—Minimal expense for portfolio management because index funds rarely need changes.
- **Performance**—With low fees they offer better performance than actively managed mutual funds.
- **May be bought on margin**—Although most investors should stay away from margin, there is an opportunity to sign up for a margin account. Mutual funds can't be bought on margin or sold short.
- **May be sold short**—Shorting is available in a margin account, but with the availability of inverse ETFs that don't require margin, that is a simpler and less expensive option because there are no margin interest charges. Bear market profits can be made using these funds because they rise when the stock market falls.

- **Useful for implementing investing/trading strategies—** Any trading/investing strategy can be used.
- **Potential for dividends and income—**Income generated using equity and fixed-income ETFs.

ETF Risks

ETFs have risks, as do all types of investments. First, there is the risk that the ETF will trade at a discount or premium to the underlying assets, similar to the way closed-end funds work. This can occur at extreme market conditions such as when trading is suspended, halted, or frozen for any number of reasons. Second, there is market risk because the ETF price changes minute-by-minute, day-by-day, and so on, just like a stock. Third, when you purchase or sell an ETF, there is the bid/ask spread (price you buy or sell an ETF at), which can be wide in low-volume ETFs or a few pennies in high-volume ETFs. If you buy ETFs in specific sectors, countries, or currencies, for example, you have the added risk of that market niche. And, lastly, if you are trying to buy an inverse fund (also known as a short fund), the shares may temporarily be unavailable, based on market conditions and exchange rules in place at the time. A situation like this occurred during the 2008–2009 financial crisis, during which there was a temporary halt in the offering of inverse financial ETFs.

Leveraged ETFs Are Very Risky and Dangerous in the Wrong Hands

Three ETF families—Rydex, ProShares, and Direxion—offer leveraged ETFs. They provide magnified returns in both up and down markets, and you can make or lose a bundle in a few days. Before discussing leveraged funds, let's first define "beta." This is a measure of risk compared to the market. For example, an ETF with a beta of "0" is not correlated to the market. However, if the beta of a fund or portfolio is 1.20, then it is 20% more volatile than the market. Likewise, a portfolio with a beta of 0.80 is 20% less volatile and is considered inversely related to the market index. As an example, the NASDAQ 2.0 beta long ETF rises 20% when the NASDAQ index rises 10%, but it falls 20% when the index drops 10%. Likewise, a NASDAQ 2.0 beta short fund goes up 20% when the NASDAQ index drops 10%, but it falls 20% when the index rises 10%. These funds are very volatile. Therefore, close monitoring with the use of limit or stop orders is necessary or losses can be huge. Of course, if you are on the right side of the market, huge gains can be attained at lightning speed. Most investors should not use these types of funds, unless all the risks are understood and the funds are used more as a hedge than for trading purposes.

There is a mathematical anomaly with leveraged ETFs that investors and traders need to understand. Because of the compounding effect and other internal fund characteristics, the leveraged funds are best used for short time frames—intraday or daily. Here is additional information on these leveraged vehicles:

- Leverage is available at factors of 1.25, 1.50, 2.00, and 3.00 beta, depending on the offering family—for example, 1.25 beta means that ETF rises or falls 25% more than the index it is tracking, and the 3.00 beta move triples the amount of the underlying index.

- Long and short (inverse) funds are available for purchase.

- Inverse ETFs are bought long and do not require a margin account.

- A number of the leveraged ETFs have unusually high trading volumes and minimal bid/ask spreads, especially the triple beta funds offered by Direxion.

- Market timers, institutions, and traders use leveraged funds.

- Inverse ETFs can be used as a hedge in a rising market. Investors can buy a certain dollar amount to keep in their portfolio, as insurance against a market drop.

In July 2009, Edward Jones, the St. Louis–based financial services firm, halted sales of leveraged ETFs by its advisors because they
consider them unsuitable for long-term investors.[8]

Also during July 2009, other firms that suspended or restricted
their advisors from soliciting leveraged ETFs included Ameriprise
Financial Inc., LPL Financial Corp., and UBS Wealth Management
Americas. Wells Fargo Advisors, Morgan Stanley, and Smith Barney
were reviewing their policies on these nontraditional ETFs. Charles
Schwab Corp. warned investors of these products' compounding
intricacies. In October 2009, JPMorgan Chase announced that it will
not permit self-directed brokerage account holders to purchase leveraged funds.

ETF Allocation for Different Investor Types

ETFs are recommended for most investors as the most appropriate way to obtain market exposure with low costs. As you know by
now, the first step is to determine your risk tolerance. This factor will
determine the appropriate percent allocation to equities and bonds.
Retirement accounts and regular brokerage accounts require a different investing approach because of the differing time frames, the
consequences of capital gains or losses, and the risk factors.

Most investors should focus on basic ETFs from the following
list for their portfolios. I recommend that a universe of 15 ETFs be
selected for your portfolios. I have provided sample allocations for
four different investor risk tolerances. For example, in the conservative allocation, 13% of the investment dollars should be placed in the
Morningstar-style ETFs and in the iShares countries. These percentages are meant to be taken as a general guide. You can make
changes as you see fit. Moreover, as you begin to see the results of

using the strategy outlined in this book, you may decide to change your initial allocations and even your investor classification to better suit your needs.

Conservative Investor Allocation

Morningstar style—13% (2 ETFs)

SPDR Sectors—13% (2 ETFs)

iShares Countries—13% (4 ETFs)

Fixed Income—54% (6 ETFs)

Specialty—7% (1 ETF)

Moderate Investor Allocation

Morningstar style—20% (3 ETFs)

SPDR Sectors—20% (3 ETFs)

iShares Countries—13% (4 ETFs)

Fixed Income—34% (3 ETFs)

Specialty—13% (2 ETFs)

Aggressive Investor Allocation

Morningstar style—20% (3 ETFs)

SPDR Sectors—20% (3 ETFs)

iShares Countries—20% (5 ETFs)

Fixed Income—20% (2 ETFs)

Specialty—20% (2 ETFs)

Very Aggressive Investor Allocation

Morningstar style—20% (3 ETFs)

SPDR Sectors—20% (3 ETFs)

iShares Countries—40% (6 ETFs)

Fixed Income—0%

Specialty—20% (3 ETFs)

Recommended ETFs

The entire ETF universe encompasses about 768 funds offered by about a dozen providers. The number of ETFs in registration for issuance is in the hundreds. However, a few of the large providers have the lion's share of the business, including BlackRock's iShares, ProShares, PowerShares, WisdomTree, and Vanguard. Obviously, there is some overlap in the popular ETF categories. For example, there are about 10 large-cap value ETFs, 8 large-cap growth, 6 mid-cap growth, 45 small funds, 11 energy funds, and 15 financials, among others. In addition, more than 140 ETFs cover U.S. industries.

ETF investments are recommended in different asset classes to provide diversification. In each asset class recommended, there are both leading and lagging ETFs as far as price performance is concerned. We want to invest in the leaders, because they tend to remain leaders for weeks or months at a time. As the leaders lose price momentum, we can then switch to those that are gaining momentum. It is as simple as that. And the details are provided so that you can do this easily on your own.

For our purposes, I've tried to select the popular, widely traded and representative ETFs. Of course you can add any of your own to the universe but be very selective. However, be cognizant that some of the international ETFs are thinly traded, resulting in bid-ask spreads that may be higher than normal. If you prefer the iShares style box ETFs over Morningstar's, go to the iShares Web site for their ticker symbols. Although inverse ETFs are provided on this listing for information purposes, the ordinary investor is *not* encouraged to use them. However, after you become more experienced as an investor and understand how these inverse ETFs work and the fact that the stock market rises 70% of the time, you may want to consider using them with 5% to 10% of your cash when a "sell" signal is given by the dashboard. Of course, these ETFs need to be monitored closely, and you should use stop loss and trailing stops, as necessary.

Following is a list of the ETFs and ticker symbols suggested for your investing universe.

Morningstar Style Box	Ticker Symbol
Large-cap growth	JKE
Large-cap core	JKD
Large-cap value	JKF
Mid-cap growth	JKH
Mid-cap core	JKG
Mid-cap value	JKI
Small-cap growth	JKK
Small-cap core	JKJ
Small-cap value	JKL

Select Sector SPDRs	Ticker Symbol
Consumer discretionary	XLY
Consumer staples	XLP
Financial	XLF
Energy	XLE
Healthcare	XLV
Industrial	XLI
Materials	XLB
Technology	XLK
Utilities	XLU

International—Country Funds*	Ticker Symbol
Chile	ECH
Emerging Markets	EEM
MSCI EAFE	EFA
Israel	EIS
Peru	EPU
Australia	EWA
Canada	EWC
Sweden	EWD
Germany	EWG
Hong Kong	EWH
Italy	EWI
Japan	EWJ
Belgium	EWK
Switzerland	EWL
Malaysia	EWM
Netherlands	EWN
Austria	EWO
Spain	EWP
France	EWQ
Singapore	EWS
Taiwan	EWT
United Kingdom	EWU
Mexico	EWW
South Korea	EWY
Brazil	EWZ

International—Country Funds°	Ticker Symbol (continued)
South Africa	EZA
FTSE-Xinhua China 25	FXI
Market Vectors Indonesia	IDX
PowerShares India	PIN
Market Vectors Russia	RSX
Thailand	THD
Turkey Invest Market	TUR

°iShares unless otherwise specificied

Fixed Income	Ticker Symbol
Barclays Aggregate Bond	AGG
Barclays Int'l Tsy Bond	BWX
Barclays Intermediate Gov't Credit	GVI
iShares iBoxx $ High Yield	HYG
iShares Barclay 7- to 10-year Treasury	IEF
iShares iBoxx $ Invest. Grade Corp. Bond	LQD
iShares S&P National Muni	MUB
iShares Barclay 1- to 3-year Treasury	SHY
iShares Barclay 10- to 20-year Treasury	TLH
iShares Barclay 20-year Treasury	TLT

Specialty Funds	Ticker Symbol
SPDR Gold Shares	GLD
iShares Silver Trust	SLV
US Oil Fund	USO
PowerShares DB Agriculture	DBA
iShares Cohen & Steers Realty Majors Index	ICF
Major Vectors Solar Energy	KWT

Inverse Funds	Ticker Symbol
ProShares Short S&P 500	SH
ProShares Short NASDAQ 100	PSQ
ProShares Short Financials	SEF
ProShares Short MSCI EAFE	EFZ
ProShares Short MSCI Emerging Markets	EUM

Benchmarks	Ticker Symbol
SPDR S&P 500 Index	SPY
PowerShares NASDAQ 100	QQQQ
Vanguard Total Stock Market	VTI

Now that we have our customized investing universe and you know *where to invest* your money, the next step is to determine *when to invest.* Unfortunately, too many investors just jump into the market when they get an investing idea, irrespective of the market's risk. The "Stock Market Dashboard" explained in the next chapter provides a gauge as to when the investing odds are in your favor. This gauge also suggests the opportune time to sell.

Appendix 4.1: Discount and Full-Service Brokerage Firms

Brokerage Firm	Web Site	Trade Commission
Charles Schwab	www.schwab.com	$8.95
E°Trade	www.etrade.com	$12.99
Fidelity	www.fidelity.com	$7.95
Interactive Brokers	www.interactivebrokers.com	$.005 per share
OptionsXpress	www.optionsxpress.com	$9.95
Scottrade	www.scottrade.com	$7.00
TD Ameritrade	www.tdameritrade.com	$9.99
Thinkorswim	www.thinkorswim.com	$9.95
TradeKing	www.tradeking.com	$4.95
Zecco Trading	www.zecco.com	$4.50

Note: Check with each firm for their pricing deals and packages before signing up.

Appendix 4.2: ETF Resources

Recommended ETF Books

Appel, Marvin. *Investing with Exchange-Traded Funds Made Easy: A Start to Finish Plan to Reduce Costs and Achieve Higher Returns, Second Edition.* FT Press, 2008.

Lydon, Tom. *The ETF Trend Following Playbook: Profiting from Trends in Bull or Bear Markets with Exchanged Traded Funds.* FT Press, 2009.

Lydon, Tom and Wasik, John F. *iMoney: Profitable ETF Strategies for Every Investor.* FT Press, 2008.

Wild, Russell. *Exchange-Traded Funds For Dummies.* For Dummies, 2006.

ETF Web Sites

www.amex.com
www.etf.com
www.etf-central.com
www.etfdb.com
www.etfguide.com
www.etfreplay.com
www.etfscreen.com
www.etftable.com
www.etftrades.com
www.etftradingstrategies.com
www.etftrends.com
www.etfxray.com
www.etfzone.com
www.finance.yahoo.com/etf
www.indexfunds.com
www.indexuniverse.com
www.marketwatch.com/tools/etfs/html-home.asp
www.morningstar.com/goto/etfs
www.sectorspdr.com

Endnotes

1 Stovall, Sam. "The Conservative Investor." *Bottom Line Retirement*, June 2009, p. 8.

2 Mamudi, Sam. "Top Mutual Funds: Just Luck or Skill?" *The Wall Street Journal*, December 3, 2009, p. C13.

3 Laise, Eleanor. "More Mutual Funds 'Time' Market." *The Wall Street Journal*, November 12, 2009.

4 Cohen, Lisa A. "It's Raining Funds!" *Registered Rep*, November 2009, p. 78.

5 Kates-Smith, Anne. "ETFs: Not So Simple Anymore." *Kiplinger's Personal Finance*, August 2009.

6 Delegge, Ronald L. "Will Active ETFs Dominate?" Researchmag.com.

7 Santoli, Michael. "Growing to the Sky." *Barron's*, October 19, 2009, p. E4.

8 "Edward Jones: No Leveraged ETFs." *The Wall Street Journal*, July 22, 2009, p. C11.

5

The Stock Market Dashboard— Key Stock Market Indicators to Gauge the Market's Direction

"Markets are never wrong; opinions are."
Jesse Livermore, speculator

"Bear markets have always been temporary. And so have bull markets..."
John Templeton, investor, philanthropist, mutual fund pioneer, and billionaire

Common Wall Street wisdom is that the trend is your friend. That is why it is important that you nail the trend so that you are on the right side of the market 100% of the time. Buying stocks in a declining market is suicide, as is shorting stocks in a rising market. Predicting where the market is headed is an impossible task, so how do you determine what to do? Simple, just listen to what the market is telling you.

There are only three possible scenarios: The market is rising, declining, or marking time in a trading range. If the trend has just turned positive, you simply hold any existing portfolios and consider adding positions with available cash. On the other hand, if the trend has just turned down, you would sell existing positions, and definitely not add new positions. Lastly, if the market is in a trading range—for example, the S&P 500 Index is fluctuating between 1,000 and 1,200 for weeks or months—then you would wait for a breakout in either direction and then look at the dashboard indicators, as spelled out in this chapter, for confirmation of the up move or down move before taking action.

Your foremost investing decision is determining when the market direction is changing. You have to be careful of investing in a whip-sawing market (goes up and down in a trading range but is not going anywhere) because that would cause too many buys and sells, result-ing in continual losses until a new trend develops. Therefore, to put the odds in your favor, I recommend that a combination of eight diverse indicators be used as a simple market gauge that signals when to buy and when to sell, and when to stay on the sidelines. This approach eliminates any emotional decision making that can wreak havoc on your portfolio's value, as well as eliminate the pesky minor whipsaws commonly occurring when you have no investing plan with specific parameters.

The approach proposed in this chapter is similar in logic to driving a car without having an accident. You need to observe the road condi-tions based on the traffic and weather, as well as obey the traffic sig-nals, so that you arrive safely at your destination. Therefore, you should tune in to the weather forecast, drive carefully, and obey the traffic lights—green, yellow, and red—so that you don't crash. The same logic applies to investing in the stock market. You need to know the market conditions, when it is safe to be invested (green light), when you should dump your portfolios (red light) to preserve your principal and avoid stock market crashes, and when to do nothing (yellow light).

Based on my decades of investing experience coupled with my research on market indicators and technical analysis, I have con-cluded that a single indicator cannot be relied on to accurately and consistently call every key turning point. There are hundreds of indicators to choose from, but many of them are redundant or don't provide much value. Nevertheless, I did find a number of indicators that, when used in combination, provide reliable buy and sell signals at major turning points. The best of the bunch have been assembled for use in the dashboard. Also, I selected indicators that are readily available free on the Internet for viewing.

You may find that using and understanding the indicators may seem daunting at first. However, after you have worked with them for a short period of time, you will find that they are easy to obtain and work with, and each will only take a few minutes of your time to view and interpret. Moreover, many of the indicators are found on www. stockcharts.com, which further reduces your search and retrieval time.

Pay No Attention to Wall Street Experts

The radio and TV airwaves are filled with Wall Street propaganda emphasizing that no one can predict the market's future direction with consistency, and that no one can time the market. It is true that no one can predict where the market is headed; however, there is no need to forecast where the market is going. That is because when the market begins to change direction, that condition can be monitored using the dashboard.

There are individual investors and professionals who can successfully time the market, although the percentage of successful timing services is probably small compared to all the services monitored. Timing services have been around for decades and many have been tracked for years by such services as *Timer Digest*, TimerTrac, and the *Hulbert Financial Digest*. Moreover, the TV and radio commentators continue to interview stock market experts and ask them for their "top picks right now"—what useless drivel. We do not know these experts' agendas for being on the program or the real reasons they may be pushing certain stocks. More important, are they going to come on the air and tell you when to sell the stocks? Probably not, as we have witnessed on many occasions.

Most likely after a recommended stock drops 90% the expert will issue a sell signal. Thanks a lot. Just think about WorldCom, Enron, Bear Stearns, Lehman Brothers, General Motors, General Electric, AIG, Citicorp, and many other companies whose stocks got demolished before analysts rated them a sell. On the other hand, an astute investor who simply used a weekly price chart with a simple 20-week moving average, for example, could have protected much of his principal in all the preceding cases by selling after the stock price pierced its moving average to the downside, even if the investor was completely unaware of the reason for the price decline.

Take a look at three of the charts for the previously mentioned companies using only the 20-week simple moving average to see my point. Selling AIG (Figure 5.1) in October 2007, Citicorp (Figure 5.2) in late June 2007, and GE (Figure 5.3) in October 2007 or in April 2008 (after the run up and price drop), when each stock price went below its 20-week, would have served investors well by avoiding the latest stock market crash that crushed the price of these stocks.

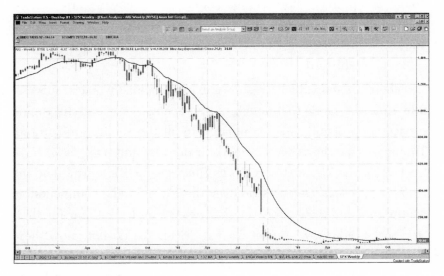

Figure 5.1   AIG chart

Created with TradeStation, which is a registered TradeStation Group, Inc. Printed with permission.

Figure 5.2   Citicorp chart

Created with TradeStation, which is a registered TradeStation Group, Inc. Printed with permission.

Figure 5.3   GE chart

Created with TradeStation, which is a registered TradeStation Group, Inc. Printed with permission.

Introducing the Stock Market Dashboard

To monitor the health of the stock market, I have developed a composite gauge called the "Stock Market Dashboard," which is composed of eight publicly available (free) indicators. The composite gauge will provide a "go" or "no-go" assessment as to whether to be a buyer or a seller of ETFs at a particular point in time. The key to profitable investing is to control and minimize market risk by putting the odds in your favor. Knowing and investing with the market's trend is critical to becoming a consistent winner in the stock market. The other option is not very pleasant and can be costly, as you and millions of other investors have discovered.

The overall direction of the stock market is the main determinant of how well your personal portfolios will perform. A number of stock market researchers have estimated that approximately 70% of an individual stock's return is a result of the stock market's overall trend, about 20% of the return is determined by the stock's industry or sector, and only 10% of the return is based on the individual stock's performance. The first question to answer is this: How do we determine the market's current trend?

Initially this chapter provides a top-down brief overview of the eight indicators. Then detailed information is provided with chart examples, and lastly a scoring system is presented to tally the signal scores. Moreover, free Internet data sources for these indicators are provided so that you can track the market's performance quickly and easily. In summary, you will have everything you need to compute the dashboard composite gauge at your fingertips. All you have to do is check the dashboard after the Friday market close or on the weekend to see where the market stands. Of course, if the market is in a trend that hasn't changed direction in the past week, you can wait until the following week to check things out, because no signal would have been triggered. When used together, the indicators will pinpoint market bottoms and tops at major market turning points with a high degree of reliability. We are looking to identify *only extreme readings* (high and low points) on each indicator (except moving averages, which have crossovers and not extreme readings) that have coincided with market index highs and lows in the past three years, and will hopefully do so in the future. But there is no guarantee that they will perform as expected going forward. Based on observation, I have found that when the composite reading reaches a +3 (out of 8) or more, that is considered a market turning point or "buy" signal to invest cash. Likewise, a –3 reading is considered a "sell" signal to liquidate your positions.

These indicators measure the internal characteristics of the market, including price action (which is the purest indicator of market strength or weakness), new highs and lows, and bullish chart patterns, among others. No fundamental data or forecasts are used in this analysis. Because all the information about the market and any security are already baked into the price, there is no reason to add extraneous information that has no value.

Three Market Entry Strategies to Consider

Here are three approaches you should consider for employing your available funds when a +3 dashboard reading (buy signal) has occurred:

1. Invest 100% of your cash funds immediately. This is the most aggressive option and provides an opportunity for the greatest profits because you are entering the market early in the expected uptrend.

2. Invest 80% with a +3 reading and then 15% more for each additional positive reading above +3. This approach gets you in the market more slowly, but involves less risk than the first choice.

3. Invest 25% with a +3 reading, and an additional 20% for each additional positive reading, except that when +7 is reached,

you'll be investing the remaining 15% of your funds, as detailed here:

25% with a +3

20% with a +4

20% with a +5

20% with a +6

15% with a +7

This is a conservative approach, in which you spread your money out in order to wait for additional confirming positive signals. Be aware that you may or may not get a +7 reading so you may want to invest the remainder of your money at +6 or +5 to make sure you do not give up too much of the move.

If you prefer to use different investment amounts on the first buy signal or subsequent signals, that is your call. Only by actually working with varying approaches with real dollars will you know what is best for you. Start out conservatively so that you feel comfortable with the approach and the amount of risk you are taking.

Sell All Equity Positions on a Dashboard Sell Signal

When a dashboard sell signal (–3) is given, you should sell all equities. This will result in having 100% cash that can be placed in cash equivalents (for example, Internet bank money market funds, money market mutual funds, or a savings account) until the next buy signal is given. When a sell signal is given, aggressive, knowledgeable, and risk-aware investors may want to buy a small position (5% to 10% of cash assets) in one of the ProShares inverse funds such as PSQ (inverse the NASDAQ 100) because it *rises* in price when the NASDAQ 100 index *falls*. I would not recommend that you buy a leveraged inverse fund because you need complete knowledge about its risks and quirky compounding. Shorting the market requires skill, nerves of steel, and the ability to cover your short position at the first sign of a rally. So in summary, you should not consider shorting the market with an inverse fund until you have years of successful investing under your belt and you know exactly what you are getting into.

Introduction to Dashboard Components

Let's first briefly describe the components of the "Stock Market Dashboard" with their key readings and rationale. (More detailed information is given after this introduction.)

1. ***Percentage of New York Stock Exchange (NYSE) Stocks Above Their 50-Day Moving Average (50-dma).*** When the percentage of NYSE stocks above their 50-dma price drops below 25%, and then reverses upward, that usually pinpoints that a market bottom has been reached. Historically, it has been a good time to invest. Likewise, when the percentage of stocks above their 50-dma is above 75% or more and then recedes, the odds indicate that a market top has probably been reached and it is time to take money off the table. I could easily have used a 20-dma or a 100-dma alternative with their appropriate buy and sell percentages, but I picked the 50-dma as a compromise. The logic for using this indicator is that when a large percentage of stocks have participated in a market rally, you should be cautious since there may not much more left in market gains. And the opposite is also true. Of course, the amount of time that stocks stay above their moving average can be extensive, but eventually they will fall below it. That is why we monitor the *extreme* readings of 25% and 75%, and not in between, and wait for a reversal in the opposite direction to the prevailing trend.

2. ***NASDAQ Composite Stock Index Crosses the 100-dma.*** When the price of any broad market index (e.g., S&P 500, NASDAQ Composite, or Wilshire 5000) pierces its 100-dma from below, that is considered a buy signal, and when it falls and

crosses the average from above, that is considered a sell signal. The logic of using this indicator is that when an index has finally crossed its medium-term moving average, the trend has probably changed and will continue in that direction for many months. We will use the NASDAQ Composite Index as the indicator of the entire stock market trend, because it generally leads the other indexes in both directions when the trend changes. Interestingly, when this index is lagging the other broad indexes, it is a sign of market weakness.

A 50-dma or a 200-dma or another alternative could have been selected. They all would work well, but there would be more whipsaws with the 50-dma because it is shorter. And the 200-dma provides later entry and exit points. The 100-dma is a good compromise. Moreover, other researchers have found that a moving average around this time frame has produced very good results. These researchers include Robert W. Colby (126-dma), Paul Merriman (100-dma), and Michael McDonald (132-dma).

3. **NYSE Daily New Highs Minus Daily New Lows.** When the difference between the number of new daily highs and the number of new daily lows reaches an *extreme number of –750* or more and then over the next few days reverses higher, that usually signifies a market low and therefore a buying opportunity because the market is considered to be washed out. The logic of using this indicator is that when the new lows overwhelm the new highs, the market typically reverses direction and keeps rising. This indicator has not provided a usable sell signal when the number of new highs is greater than the number of new lows. Instead look at the actual number of *weekly* new NYSE highs divided by the total number of issues traded that week. This provides a good gauge of a potential market high. When that percentage reaches 25% *to* 30% and then drops in the following week or two, that is a good sign that a market high has been seen.

4. ***NYSE Bullish Percentage (NYSEBP) on a Point-and-Figure Chart.*** This indicator provides the number of stocks whose point-and-figure chart patterns are on buy signals. When this number peaks above 70% and starts to drop, that is considered a sell signal. Likewise, when this number falls to 30% or below and starts to turn up, that is a buy signal, as the market low has probably been reached. Point-and-figure charts are unusual charts compared to the standard bar and candlestick charts. The logic of this indicator is that when an overwhelming number of stocks have bullish chart patterns, the market probably has reached a high point. When the percentage of stocks exhibiting that pattern drops from that level, that is the time to sell. The opposite is also true since a low reading is most likely a market low point.

5. ***MACD (Moving Average Convergence-Divergence) Indicator Reading on the NASDAQ Composite Index.*** This trending technical indicator's signal is based on a MACD line, composed of the 26-day exponential moving average subtracted from the 12-day exponential moving average crossing over a MACD Signal Line (the 9-day exponential moving average of the MACD). This crossover pinpoints buy and sell signals on any stock, ETF, or market index. We will use the NASDAQ Composite Index to represent the overall market with the MACD measuring its changing direction. The logic of this indicator is that when these two lines cross each other, the market's trend has changed direction.

6. ***AAII Weekly Investor Sentiment Survey Bullish Percentage.*** The majority of investors typically have an incorrect view of the market's future direction at the key turning points. Therefore, the weekly readings of the American Association of Individual Investors (AAII) survey of its individual members will be used to look for extremely bullish (50% or more) or mildly bullish readings (25% or lower). These two extreme

readings provide a *contrary view* of the market. The logic of this indicator is that when the investor sentiment reading is extremely bullish, that is a probable sign of a market top, and vice versa. When the percentage reaches 50% and then drops lower (to 40%, for example) in the following week, that is an indication of a market top; and when the reading is 25% or lower and turns up in the next week, that is an indication of a market bottom.

7. ***Best-Six-Months Strategy with the MACD Indicator.*** Using this well-known strategy developed by Yale Hirsch, an investor would be continuously invested from November 1 to April 30 of each year, and then be in cash for the remaining six months. According to *The Stock Trader's Almanac 2010,* going back to 1950, investing $10,000 on November 1, 1950, in the Dow Jones Industrial Average aggregated to $463,305 at the end of April 2008, more than 57 times the return of the other six-month period. Coupling this strategy with the previously mentioned MACD indicator to tweak these dates based on an MACD buy or sell signal provided almost triple the return for the same time frame. This strategy does not work well every year, but overall it has good results for its simplicity of two signals a year.

8. ***NASDAQ Summation Index (NASI) Moving Average Crossover with MACD Indicator Confirmation.*** The NAS-DAQ Summation Index is mathematically derived from the number of advancing and declining issues in the NASDAQ Composite Index. When it is rising and the index crosses its five-day exponential moving average (ema), that is a sell signal. Likewise, when it rises through its five-day ema on the upside, that is a buy signal. Also included on the NASI chart is the NASDAQ Composite Index for comparison purposes and the MACD for confirmation purposes. The logic of this indicator is that when the number of advancing issues or declining issues reaches an extreme point, a sell or buy signal will be given.

Detailed Indicator Review

Now that you've been briefly introduced to the dashboard components, let's review them in more detail, with their accompanying charts so you can understand how easy it is to spot the changing trend.

1. Percentage of NYSE Stocks Above Their 50-Day Moving Average

When the stock market gets overheated and reaches lofty levels, it is time to pay attention to a possible stall or change in direction. Likewise, after the stock market has dropped a significant percentage (30% to 50%) in price, a reversal may be imminent. Referring to the chart in Figure 5.4, you can observe that when the percentage of stocks above their own 50-dma rises above 75% and starts to fall, that is usually, but not always, a market high. It may not be the ultimate peak of the bull market, but it is still at a lofty level and you should be prepared to take profits or at least cash in a percentage of your profits as long as a sell signal is generated by the composite reading of the dashboard.

In late February 2007, after the percentage of stocks peaked at 78% and started to decline, the stock market took a quick hit. The indicator rose from a spike low of 30% in early March 2007 and kept on going up during April and May of 2007. There were numerous times when this indicator dropped to below 25% and reversed up (August, November, and December 2007; January, March, July, and October–November 2008; and March and July 2009). Those were all low points in the index readings. Likewise, there were numerous times when the indicator rose above 75% and reversed down, including June and October 2007; March 2008; and January, May, and August 2009. These were all high points for the index and good sell signals.

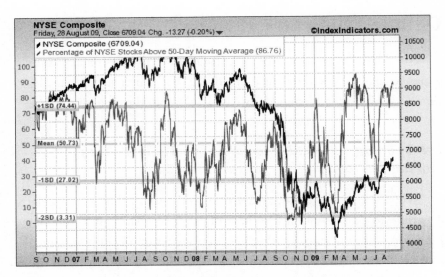

Figure 5.4   Percentage of NYSE stocks above their 50-day moving average

Source: indexindicators.com

The high readings above 80% and one reading at 95% during April through June 2009 could not be sustained for long, and we did see a pullback to a reading of 30% before the next leg up took off to new highs in August, September, and October (not on the chart).

2. NASDAQ Composite Stock Index Crosses the 100-dma

Many professional traders, money managers, and individual investors observe the market's performance in relationship to its long-term 200-day moving average to ascertain whether the market is in a bullish or bearish mode. I used the 100-dma instead because it offers quicker buy and sell signals, and produces more profit in both up and down markets. When the price of the index closes above its 100-dma, that is considered bullish, and vice versa. This moving average smoothes the price of the index for the past 100 days and plots each day's value as a point. All the points are connected as a smoothed line.

Simply adding the price of the index for the past 100 trading days and dividing by 100 calculates it. That gives the value of the moving average for today and is the last point on the moving average line. That same calculation is done daily, dropping off the 101st day.

For illustrative purposes, the 200-dma and 100-dma lines were both placed on the chart shown in Figure 5.5. But I will focus my comments mostly on the 100-dma. This is the top moving average line on the chart in 2007 that turns into the lower line thereafter. You can observe that the first sell signal came in August 2007, followed by multiple whipsaws above and below the 100-dma until a clear buy signal occurred in September 2007, then a few more whipsaws above and below the moving average line, and finally a sell signal at the end of 2007. The next buy signal was not given until April 2008 and then a subsequent sell signal came in late June 2008. Then there were a few more whipsaws in August and a final sell signal in early September 2008. That sell signal was at NASDAQ 2400.

Subsequently, the NASDAQ dropped 48% to 1250 on March 9, 2009, and those who used this moving average approach were safely and happily out of the market. The next buy signal was in early April 2009 at NASDAQ 1500, to take advantage of the next huge rally. As you can see, the 200-dma was not crossed to the upside by the index until NASDAQ 1700 in late May.

Whipsaws are defined as buy and sell signals near a moving average. They can be numerous when the market is in a trading range as it was July and August, and November and December 2007. That is why this indicator should not be used in isolation—buying and selling frequently near the moving average can be costly in commissions and lost principal if you keep on being knocked out of the market until the true trend develops. Using the composite dashboard reading will avoid too many unprofitable whipsaw transactions.

Of course, you can choose any moving average you want, but the shorter the length, the more transactions and whipsaws will occur. So it is a trade-off as to which moving average you use.

Figure 5.5   NASDAQ Composite Stock Index crosses the 100-day moving average

Chart provided courtesy of stockcharts.com.

I felt that the 100-dma was more reasonable than the 200-dma or the 50-dma. You can see that the 200-dma did not get you back in the market until late May 2009, almost two months after the 100-dma already gave a buy signal in early April 2009.

3. NYSE Daily New Highs Minus Daily New Lows

This chart depicts the number of new daily highs minus the number of new lows and plots the difference daily. As you can observe in the chart shown in Figure 5.6, when the difference was more than –750 and the number reversed up to a lower low (for example, from –750 to –700), that signals a market bottom. The NYSE Composite Index is shown on the upper chart. You can see that the lows in this index coincide with the low readings in the indicator. When –750 or lower readings occurred (January, July, September, October, and November 2008; and March 2009) and then reversed up, the NYSE Index quickly reversed direction to the upside as well. This indicator does *not* provide any usable signal when the number of new highs is greater than the number of new lows. However, looking at the actual number of *weekly new highs divided by the total number of issues traded that week* provides a good gauge of a potential market high. When that percentage reaches 25% *to 30%* and then drops in the following week or two, that is a good sign that a market high has been seen. These numbers are readily available in *Barron's* and many Internet sites, including http://finance.yahoo.com.

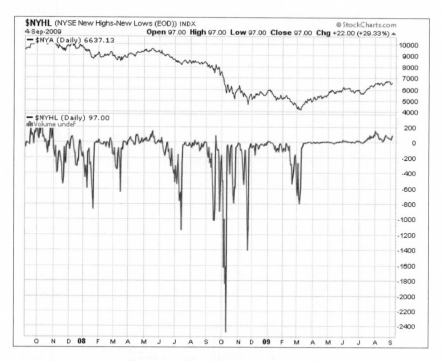

Figure 5.6   NYSE daily new highs minus daily new lows

Chart provided courtesy of stockcharts.com.

4. NYSE Bullish Percentage (NYSEBP) on a Point-and-Figure Chart

You may not be familiar with this indicator unless you use point-and-figure charts in addition to the more common bar and candlestick charts. The NYSEBP tallies the number of NYSE stocks whose point-and-figure chart patterns are on a buy signal, and expresses the number as a percentage of all listed NYSE stocks. This data can easily be obtained from a number of free sources so that we do not have to do any calculations, just analyze the chart. When the percentage of stocks reaches above 70% and turns down, that is typically a sell signal since most stocks have run up in price to unsustainable levels. Likewise, when this percentage drops to 30% or below and starts to turn up, that is the time to invest since most stocks have reached their low points. Refer to Figure 5.7 for a chart of the NYSE Bullish Percentage.

The point-and-figure chart is composed of x's and o's and takes into account only changes in price, irrespective of volume and time. Numerous books and Internet sites can provide an explanation of these types of charts, a topic that is beyond the scope of this book. All you need to know about these charts is how to identify the turning points, as previously mentioned, by simply observing the chart.

This chart indicates that the last reading in August 2009 is above 80. This reading will eventually decline, indicating that a market high has been reached. Note that this reading of 80 has not been reached since 2001 (the beginning of this chart), so it is a quite rare occurrence. Look for the first time that a column of o's appears on the chart to give you a good indication of a market top.

The market lows in 2008 and 2009 can easily be seen where the column of o's switched to a column of x's from below a reading of 30%. When the market is advancing, x's are used to show that it is rising, and when the market starts to fall, o's are used to show the change in direction.

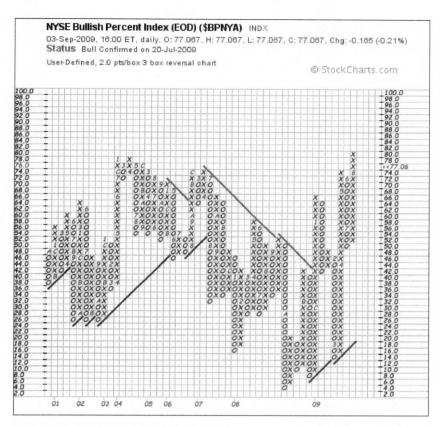

Figure 5.7   NYSE Bullish Percentage

Chart provided courtesy of stockcharts.com.

The numbers 1–9 on the chart represent the first ten months of the year (1 = January, 2 = February, etc.), and the letters represent October through December (A = October, B = November, C = December).

5. AAII Weekly Investor Sentiment Survey Bullish Percentage

Individual investors are consistently bearish at market bottoms and bullish at market tops. This is due to the emotional attachment

that investors have with their stocks and how they interpret the financial and world news. They panic near bottoms and become euphoric
at market tops. The American Association of Individual Investors
(AAII) tracks its membership's opinions weekly on where they believe
the market is headed over the next six months. The numbers are tabulated and released each Thursday morning.

High bullish readings of 50% or more, followed by a decline, typically denote a peak in stock prices, and low bullish readings of 25%
or less that increase denote market low points. The chart shown in
Figure 5.8 illustrates the bullish sentiment readings from 2005 forward compared to the S&P 500 Index on the top portion of the chart.
You can readily see that the peaks and troughs of the sentiment index
mirror the same points on the index. The AAII percent bullish
reached 50% in late August 2009 (not seen on the chart), May 2008,
October 2007, and January 2007, all market high points. For further
information about the index, contact the American Association of
Individual Investors (www.aaii.com).

6. MACD Indicator Reading on the NASDAQ Composite Index

This trend-following technical indicator was developed by Gerald
Appel. The MACD is calculated by subtracting the slower 26-day
exponential moving average from the faster 12-day exponential moving average of an index, stock, or ETF. The MACD Signal line is a
nine-period EMA of the MACD. When the MACD line crosses the
signal line in either direction, that is considered a buy or sell signal. A
cross from below is a buy signal and vice versa. Exponential averages
place more weight on the more recent data and typically provide
quicker signals than simple moving averages.

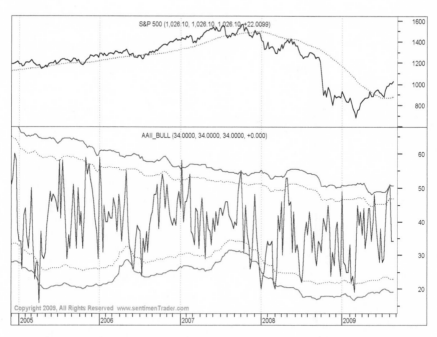

Figure 5.8   AAII Weekly bullish investor sentiment readings

Printed with permission of www.sentimenTrader.com. Data provided to SentimenTrader by the American Association of Individual Investors (AAII).

Refer to the chart in Figure 5.9, which shows the NASDAQ Composite Index with a 50-day simple moving average and the MACD indicator just below it. When the MACD line crosses the signal line to the upside, as it did in mid-July 2008, at the end of October 2008, late November 2008, and mid-March 2009, those were considered buy signals. Among the sell signals given were mid-August 2008, late November 2008, early January 2009, and mid-February 2009. However, some of those buy and sell signals lasted only a short time because of the rapidly moving markets. Again, that is why using only

one indicator, like this one, to make a buy or sell decision is not prudent, and would result in numerous commissions for buying and
selling.

Figure 5.9   NASDAQ Composite with the MACD indicator

Chart provided courtesy of stockcharts.com.

One interesting and powerful use of the MACD indicator is
*finding a divergence between the MACD direction compared to the
price of the index.* For example, when the MACD reading hits a low
and moves higher while the price is moving lower, that indicates a
possible price trend reversal. This is clearly shown in Figure 5.9.
From October 2008 to December 2008, the MACD was making
higher highs (from a reading of –100 to –50) while the NASDAQ
Composite was tanking. Sure enough, the composite then surged
from 1300 to 1650, indicating that the MACD divergence was an

accurate call. The early March 2009 MACD buy signal nailed the market low. And about two weeks later the NASDAQ composite price pierced its 50-dma for an additional buy signal (an indicator not in our composite). The MACD gave the buy signal well before that moving average did. If we had used a 100-dma (a slower moving average than the 50-dma), the 100-dma moving average signal would have come a few weeks later. The earlier we get multiple signals, the earlier we can enter or exit the market, providing higher returns.

7. Best-Six-Months Strategy with the MACD Indicator

Interestingly, certain months have a better stock market price performance than other months as measured over the past 50 years. According to Sam Stovall, Chief Investment Strategist, S&P Equity Research, since 1945 the S&P 500 Index has advanced an annual average of 6.6% in the November through April time frame, while a comparable investment in the May through October period generated an average annual return of only 1.4%. Moreover, the prior period has beaten the latter period 71% of the time. During the period from April 30, 1990 through October 30, 2009, four out of the ten S&P sectors have had their best performance in the November through April period—Materials (9.7% annual return), Consumer Discretionary (9.2%), Information Technology (8.5%), and Industrials (7.9%).[1] This historical performance should be kept in mind when using our relative strength approach.

Yale Hirsch, founder of *Stock Trader's Almanac*, developed the Best-Six-Months Strategy, which postulated that buying a stock index like the Dow Jones Industrial Average on November 1 of each year and selling on April 30 of the next year produces better results than being invested in the subsequent six-month period of May 1 through October 30. All you do is stay safely in cash equivalents for May 1 through October 30. Surprisingly, the basic six-month strategy has been tested on stock markets throughout the world over long time frames, and the results have been similar to Hirsch's findings.

According to Hirsch's publication, *Stock Trader's Almanac 2010*, going back to 1950, investing $10,000 for the six-month period beginning on November 1, 1950, in the Dow Jones Industrial Average aggregated to $463,305 at the end of April 2008, or a 7.3% annualized gain. On the other hand, investing $10,000 for the six-month period from May 1, 1951, to October 31, 2008, resulted in a final value of a measly $8,012 or a loss of 0.1% a year, quite a difference. And the best part is that the risk of investing was reduced by 50%, since you were in cash for May 1 through October 30 every year. This strategy is not perfect because the November–May period actually lost money in 14 years since 1950, including 2007 (–8%) and 2008 (–12.4%), but overall the results were excellent on a risk-adjusted basis. By being out of the market from the May 2007 to October 2008 period, you would have avoided a loss of 27.3%.

Sy Harding, publisher of *Street Smart Report*, further enhanced this strategy by applying the MACD indicator to tweak the buying and selling dates instead of using Hirsch's fixed dates. According to *Stock Trader's Almanac 2010*, using Harding's MACD strategy with its own tweaking and investing from the November 1 to April 30 period with a trigger of the MACD indicator produced an ending value of $1,338,258 over the same period since 1950 with an annual gain of 9.2%, while the May 1 through October 31 period with the MACD trigger ended with a value of $2,793, or a loss of $7,207, for an annual loss of –1.8%. Obviously, the inclusion of the MACD indicator almost tripled Hirsch's original approach. This MACD strategy did have nine down years during the November to April time frame. Keep in mind that the actual buy and sell dates could vary by about a month from the original dates, depending on when the MACD signal is triggered.

Presented in Table 5.1 are Sy Harding's results from 1999 to 2008 using the MACD and the Best-Six-Months Strategy (referred to as STS or Seasonal Timing System) compared to buy-and-holding the NASDAQ Composite, the S&P 500 Index, and the Dow Jones Industrial Average. His strategy beat buy-and-hold handily over three, five, and ten years. Not bad for being invested 50% of the time. Just following this strategy in 2008 proved its value and would have saved investors a great deal of money if acted on as a separate and unique strategy. Although the strategy lost 3.6% for 2008, that was much better than the 31% to 41% losses sustained by the three major indexes. The strategy has not performed well in 2009 because a May sell signal resulted in missing a large percentage of the subsequent advance through October. Keep in mind that this strategy performed poorly in 2003 as the May sell signal was wrong as the market took off. That is why, as previously mentioned, no one indicator should be used in isolation.

TABLE 5.1   Best-Six-Months Strategy Using MACD Signals 1999–2008

Year	NASDAQ	S&P 500	DJIA	STS Using DJIA Index Fund
1999 (Bull Market)	+85.6%	+20.1%	+26.8%	**+35.1%**
2000 (Bear Market)	−39.3%	−9.1%	−4.6%	**+2.1%**
2001 (Bear Market)	−21.1%	−11.9%	−5.3%	**+11.1%**
2002 (Bear Market)	−31.5%	−22.1%	−14.7%	**+3.1%**
2003 (Bull Market)	+50.0%	+28.7%	+27.6%	**+11.2%**
2004 (Bull Market)	+8.6%	+10.9%	+5.5%	**+8.1%**
2005 (Bull Market)	+1.4%	+4.8%	+1.6%	**+0.6%**
2006 (Bull Market)	+9.5%	+15.4%	+18.5%	**+14.2%**
2007 (Bull Market)	+9.8%	+5.4%	+8.6%	**+11.2%**
2008 (Bear Market)	−40.5%	−36.1%	−31.3%	**−3.6%**

Data includes dividends and interest on cash.

10-Year Return	−28.0%	−13.2%	+17.9%	**+132.5%**
5-Year Return	−21.2%	−9.6%	−5.2%	**+47.2%**
3-Year Return	−28.5%	−22.3%	−11.6%	**+22.4%**

Source: The Street Smart Report Online. Printed with permission.

The chart shown in Figure 5.10 of the S&P 500 Index and the MACD indicator provides insight on the May and November readings. For example, in late October 2008, the MACD buy signal was given very near the market lows for the year. But the MACD sell signal in May 2009 did not work out well because the market went on an upward trend after the July bottom. Because there is a risk of loss of principal if the MACD buy signal is given at the appropriate time but then turns down before the six months is up, I recommend that an additional criteria be put in place. That is, if after an October /November MACD buy signal is given and then the market turns down resulting a MACD crossover (sell signal), then the signal value should be reduced to a "0" for all remaining months in the normally favorable period. The next buy signal would not be available until the favorable period begins (the following October/November period) confirmed by a new MACD buy signal.

Figure 5.10   S&P 500 Index and the MACD indicator

Chart provided courtesy of stockcharts.com.

Likewise, after a May MACD sell signal is given and the market rises resulting in an MACD crossover (buy signal) during the unfavorable six month period, the value of the MACD sell signal would be changed to "0" for the remaining months of the unfavorable period. In looking at Figure 5.10 the May 2009 MACD sell signal was negated by the first MACD buy signal in June 2009, meaning that from that date forward the MACD signal value would be assigned a "0" weighting for all the months going forward in the unfavorable period, no matter if it then gave additional sell signals during the remaining unfavorable period.

Be Cautious in September

September has been the worst performing month of the year, showing an average –1.1% loss since 1900, according to Ned Davis Research. Just think about nasty events occurring in past Septembers, such as September 11, 2001, the Lehman and stock market collapse in September 2008, and the Long-Term Capital Management failure in September 1998. *So if the dashboard ever indicates a composite buy signal in September, be extra careful.* Interestingly, since 1900 the best performing months have been December (+1.5%), April (+1.2%), and July (+.3%). In addition, November and January tend to be fairly good months as well.

In summary, using the MACD indicator with the Best-Six-Months Strategy pinpoints the specific dates for the favorable and unfavorable periods. During the favorable time frame, each month will be given a +1 rating, and during the unfavorable months, each month will be given a –1 rating. During times when the signal is cancelled by a reversing MACD signal during the favorable or unfavorable period, respectively, it is given a "0" rating for the remainder of the months in that period. This will eliminate any erroneous signals (only determined after the fact) for the remainder of either the favorable or unfavorable period.

8. NASDAQ Summation Index Moving Average Crossover with MACD Indicator Confirmation

The NASDAQ Summation Index (NASI) is a mathematically derived value based on the number of advancing and declining stocks in the NASDAQ Composite Index. In the chart shown in Figure 5.11, you will notice that when the NASI line crosses below its five-day exponential moving average (ema), that is considered a sell signal. Likewise, when the NASI line rises through its five-day ema on the upside, that is considered a buy signal. Also included on the chart is the NASDAQ Composite Index for comparison purposes, as well as the previously discussed MACD indicator that presents a smoother line and fewer buy and sell signals than the NASI does. For our purposes, a MACD crossover needs to confirm the NASI crossover to be considered a valid buy or sell signal. As you can observe, the MACD crossover confirmed the NASI crossover buy signal in late October 2008, the sell signal in January 2009, the buy signal in mid-March 2009, the sell signal in early May 2009, the buy signal in early July 2009, and the sell signal in late August 2009. The MACD indicator did not confirm the NASI sell signal in November 2008 nor the early February 2009 and June buy signals. Compared to the highs and lows in the NASDAQ Composite Index, this MACD indicator's confirming signals to the NASI were on target with three fewer whipsaws.

Moreover, compare the NASI and the MACD in late November through early December 2008. You will notice that *both showed a positive divergence* (higher highs) compared to the NASDAQ Composite price line, which was still declining. That is interpreted as a very *strong buy signal*. Remember, MACD positive or negative divergences are one of the strongest signals to look for.

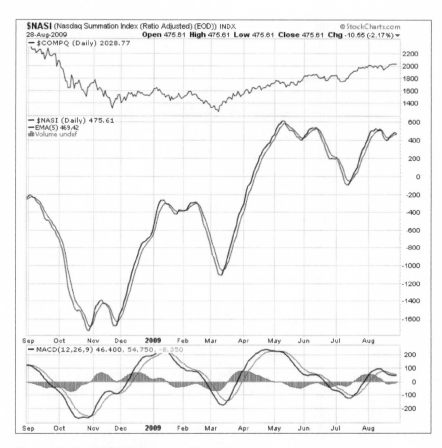

Figure 5.11   NASDAQ Summation Index

Chart provided courtesy of stockcharts.com.

Scoring System for Indicators

Now that we've reviewed the basket of indicators to determine market direction, we need to set up a scorecard indicating when each indicator gives a buy or sell signal based on our specific criteria. A weighting (assigned value) of +1 or –1 is assigned for a buy signal and sell signal, respectively. Then we add up all the assigned values to see the total value that can range between a –8 (most bearish) to a +8 (most bullish). A composite reading of –2 to +2 is indeterminate and should not be acted on. A majority of three signals in either direction determines whether we have a composite buy or sell signal. When you reach +3, that is the time to put a large portion of your money to work. As more positive signals trigger, you can incrementally add the remainder of your available funds.

Likewise, when a dashboard sell signal of –3 or more is registered, you would exit the market with all your equity positions and place the proceeds in a money market fund or cash equivalents until the next dashboard buy signal is generated. There is no need to wait for additional sell signals to trigger because this may lead to further deterioration in your portfolio's value.

Number of Yearly Buy and Sell Signals

Recognize that none of the individual dashboard indicators presented is flawless by itself, and no one indicator should be used to make investment decisions. When a majority of the indicators are going in the same direction, this indicates that the odds are heavily in your favor that the market direction has changed. Also, remember that there could be whipsaws causing the composite signal to switch to buy from sell in a short time frame. However, our indicator parameters have been set at extreme readings, so the number of whipsaws should be greatly minimized. Overall you should expect between one to two buy signals and the same number of sell signals, per year on average, but there may be times when this number is exceeded. Just follow the signals religiously so that you will be there when the market is making a major trend change. If you decide to take only some buy and sell signals and not others because of outside influences, then don't bother using this approach because you will not get good results.

For your added protection, it is always important to have a defensive plan ready in case the market suddenly falls after a composite dashboard buy signal is given. That is why you need to place a stop-loss order on each ETF position in your portfolio, as soon as it is bought. You can consider this action as having portfolio insurance in case of an unexpected market tumble. The key is to protect principal at all costs. You can always reenter the market if it reverses and the dashboard issues a buy signal. These occurrences should be rare, but at least you will have added protection.

Indicator Scoring and Spreadsheet Preparation

All the indicators in the dashboard are presented here with their chart setting, buy and sell signal criteria, buy and sell values, and primary and secondary information sources. When the signal triggers, a value of +1 or –1 is assigned to it depending on whether it is a buy or sell signal. Remember the special case for the MACD signal for the Best-Six-Months Strategy where a value of "0" is applied if either the buy or sell signal is reversed in its favorable or unfavorable period, respectively. That is one of the cases where a "0" is assigned in our scoring system.

I suggest that you prepare a spreadsheet with the indicators listed on the left side followed by a "TOTAL" line and the dates for consecutive Friday across the top. Every week you should review these indicators and record any change in the readings. This allows you to see any weakening or strengthening indicators over time and alerts you ahead of time to a potential signal change. This process should take you about five minutes once it is all set up. Be aware that although the charts from stockcharts.com are free, you cannot save them as favorites, as the site does not allow it. However, if you do not want to set up each chart from scratch each week, then you may want to subscribe for a year to their $14.95/month service that allows you to save screens and provides many other useful features. Check out the different subscription plans on the site. Even if you decide not to subscribe, you will gain proficiency in quickly bringing up the charts over time, and after a month or so, you'll be a pro.

1. Percentage of NYSE Stocks Above Their 50-Day Moving Average

Chart setting: Daily.

Buy signal: Percentage drops to 25% or below and reverses up.

Sell signal: Percentage reaches 75% or above and reverses down.

Buy signal value: +1.

Sell signal value: −1.

Source of free chart: http://stockcharts.com. Click the Free Charts tab at the top of the home page. In the Sharp Charts section at the top center of the page type $nya50R as the ticker symbol and click go to bring up the chart. Leave all settings.

Additional source: Go to: http://beta.barchart.com/stocks/momentum.php. You will find the data in the first table labeled 50-dma.

2. NASDAQ Composite Stock Index Crosses the 100-dma

Chart setting: Daily.

Buy signal: Price of the index rises from below and crosses above its moving average line.

Sell signal: Price of the index drops below a high point and crosses its moving average line in a downward direction.

Buy signal value: +1.

Sell signal value: −1.

Source of free chart: http://stockcharts.com. Click the Free Charts tab at the top of the home page. In the Sharp Charts section at the top center of the page type $Compq as the ticker symbol and click Go to bring up the chart. Under Chart Attributes, select Periods,

Daily; Range, 2 years; Size, 620. Change the first Overlay box to 100 Simple Mov. Avg., and change all Indicators to None by scrolling through the choices. Then click on Update to get the chart.

Other free charts: http://bigcharts.com; http://finance.yahoo.com; www.freestockcharts.com. You'll need to navigate these sites to find the information.

3. NYSE Daily New Highs Minus Daily New Lows

Chart setting: Daily.

Buy signal: Difference between the number of daily new highs and the number of daily new lows. When this difference reaches –750 or lower and reverses up it is a buy signal.

Sell signal: None for this specific indicator because there is no consistency when it's above 0. Instead, access *Barron's* Market Laboratory section in its paper edition, and on the right side of the page is a Trading Diary heading where you'll find the *weekly* data in the second section, Weekly Comp. Then take the number of *weekly new highs and divide it by the total issues traded that week*. When that number reaches 25% and starts dropping, that is a sell signal.

Buy signal value: +1.

Sell signal value: –1. You can use the paper edition of *Barron's* or the online version if you are a subscriber.

Neutral signal: 0 (assigned exactly 6 months after initial signal, if there is no new signal).

Source of free chart: http://stockcharts.com. Click the Free Charts tab at the top of the home page. In the Sharp Charts section at the top center of the page put in $NYHL as the ticker symbol and click Go to open the chart. Under Chart Attributes select Periods, Daily; Range, 2 years; Size, 620. Go to the Indicators section and in the first line scroll up to "price," which is the second from the top on the list, and type $NYA (New York Stock Exchange Composite Index). Then click Update to get the chart. The $NYA will be on the top of the chart and the $NYHL indicator will be under it.

Other free charts or data: http://online.wsj.com (click the Markets tab, then click Market Center), http://finance.yahoo.com, and many other sources. All you are looking for is the number of daily NYSE highs and lows for each week, so you don't necessarily need a chart.

Source of new highs: Use *Barron's* online or paper edition or free public edition at http://online.barrons.com/mktlab and click on Trading Diary. Data is under chart.

4. NYSE Bullish Percentage on a Point-and-Figure Chart

Chart setting: Daily.

Buy signal: Percentage falls to 30% or below and starts to turn up.

Sell signal: Percentage peaks above 70% and starts to turn down.

Buy signal value: +1.

Sell signal value: –1.

Neutral signal: 0 (assigned exactly 6 months after initial signal, if there is no new signal).

Source of free chart: http://stockcharts.com. Click the Free Charts tab at the top of the home page. In the Sharp Charts section at the top center of the page, type $BPNYA as the ticker symbol and click Go to bring up the chart. Then go to the bottom of that page below the Indicators section and look for the Point and Figure Chart link. Click it and the chart will appear with x's and o's.

5. MACD (Moving Average Convergence-Divergence) Indicator Reading on the NASDAQ Composite Index

Chart setting: Daily.

Buy signal: Price of lower MACD line rises from below and crosses the other MACD line.

Sell signal: Price of the higher MACD line declines and crosses the other MACD line from above.

Buy signal value: +1.

Sell signal value: –1.

Neutral signal: 0 (assigned exactly 6 months after initial signal, if there is no new signal).

Source of free chart: http://stockcharts.com. Click the Free Charts tab at the top of the home page. In the Sharp Charts section at the top center of the page, type $Compq as the ticker symbol and click Go to bring up the chart. Under Chart Attributes, select Periods, Daily; Range, 2 years; Type, Candlesticks; Size, 620. Also, leave the first of the three Overlay items as 50-dma Simple Mov. Avg.; change the second Overlay to None by scrolling up in that box until None appears; for Indicators, change RSI to None by scrolling up in that box; leave the second Indicator as MACD; and then click Update to get the chart.

Other free sources: Many other sites contain basic charting with MACD as an optional indicator, such as http://bigcharts.com, http://finance.yahoo.com, and www.cnbc.com.

6. AAII Weekly Investor Sentiment Survey Bullish Percentage

Chart setting: Weekly.

Buy signal: The bullish percentage drops to 25% and then rises the next week.

Sell signal: The bullish percentage rises to 50% and then drops the next week.

Buy signal value: +1.

Sell signal value: –1.

Neutral signal: 0 (assigned exactly 6 months after initial signal, if there is no new signal).

Sources of data: *Barron's* paper edition (on the "Market Laboratory—Indicators" page look for "Investor Sentiment Readings") in the middle of the page where you will find the AAII Index readings listed for the latest week and two weeks prior; www.aaii.com (go to the home page, scroll down in the middle of the page, and find Senti-

ment Survey to access current and past readings); www.decisionpoint.
com (subscription).

Source of our chart: www.sentimenTrader.com (subscription).

7. Best-Six-Months Strategy with MACD Indicator

Chart setting: Daily. Use Standard & Poor's 500 Stock Index with
the MACD indicator.

Buy signal: Price of the lower MACD moving average line rises
from below and crosses the other MACD moving average line after
mid-October forward.

Sell signal: Price of the higher MACD moving average declines
and crosses the lower MACD moving average line from above from
late to mid-April forward.

Buy signal value: +1 continuous for the next six-months until an
MACD sell signal occurs during the unfavorable period. *However*, if
an MACD sell crossover occurs any time during the favorable six
months after the initial buy signal, then that sell signal would negate
the earlier buy signal and the indicator value should be set to "0" for
the remaining months.

Sell signal value: −1 continuous for the next six months until a buy
signal occurs at or near May. *However*, if an MACD buy crossover
occurs at any time during this period after the sell signal was given,
then signal value should be changed to "0" negating the prior sell signal for the remaining months.

Source of free chart: http://stockcharts.com. Click the Free
Charts tab at the top of the home page. In the Sharp Charts section at
the top center of the page, type $SPX as the ticker symbol and click
Go. Under Chart Attributes Period, select Daily; Range, 2 years;
Type, Candlesticks; Size, 620. In the first Overlay section leave the
50-dma Simple Mov. Avg.; change the second Overlay to None by
scrolling up in that box for the word None; in the Indicators section
change RSI to None by scrolling up in that box; leave the second
Indicator as MACD; and then click Update to get the chart.

Other free sources: Many other sites contain basic charting with MACD as an optional indicator, such as http://bigcharts.com, http://finance.yahoo.com, and www.cnbc.com.

8. NASDAQ Summation Index Moving Average Crossover with MACD Indicator Confirmation.

Chart setting: Daily.

Buy signal: Price of index rises through its 5-day ema moving from below and the MACD has a confirming buy signal near or on that day.

Sell signal: Price of index drops below its 5-day ema from above and the MACD has a confirming sell signal near or on that day.

Buy signal value: +1.

Sell signal value: −1.

Source of free chart: http://stockcharts.com. Click the Free Charts tab at the top of the home page. In the Sharp Charts section at the top center of the page, type $NASI as the ticker symbol and click Go. Under Chart Attributes Period, select Daily; Range, 1 Year; Type, leave as is; Size, 620. Also, change the first Overlay to Exp. Mov. Avg. and change its Parameter to 5; change the second Overlay to None by scrolling up in that box; for the first Indicator change RSI to Price by scrolling up in that box; opposite Price type $compq, the symbol for NASDAQ Composite, and then for Position scroll down and select Behind Price; leave the second Indicator as MACD; and finally click Update to get the chart.

Quick Reference Guide to Dashboard Signals

A summary of the critical dashboard information in table format is provided so that you can photocopy it for your quick reference and use.

TABLE 5.2   Quick Reference Guide to Eight Dashboard Signals

Indicator Name	Critical High/Low Levels	Assigned Value
1. Percentage of NYSE Stocks Above Their 50-Day Moving Average	Less than 25% then rises	+1
	Greater than 75% then falls	−1
2. NASDAQ Composite Stock Index Crosses 100-Day Moving Average	Index crosses MA from below	+1
	Index crosses MA from above	−1
3. NYSE New *Daily* Highs Minus New *Daily* Lows	−750 or more and recedes	+1
Weekly New Highs as % of Total Issues Traded	25%+ and then declines	−1
	No signal change for 6 months	0
4. NYSE Bullish Percentage	Less than 30% and turns higher	+1
	More than 70% and declines	−1
	No signal change for 6 months	0
5. NASDAQ Composite with MACD	MACD crossover to upside	+1
	MACD crossover to downside	−1
6. AAII Weekly Investor Sentiment Survey Bullish Percentage	Less than 25% and turns higher	+1
	More than 50% and turns lower	−1
	No signal change for 6 months	0
7. Best-Six-Months Strategy with MACD	MACD crossover up near November on S&P 500 Index	+1
November through April	MACD crossover down near May on S&P 500 Index	−1
May through October	A Reversal of MACD Buy or Sell Signal	0
8. NASDAQ Summation Index MA Crossover with MACD Confirmation	Price pierces 5-day ema to upside + MACD crossover at or near same date	+1
	Price pierces 5-day ema to down-side + MACD crossover at or near same date	−1

Guidance in Effective Use of the Dashboard

The use of the Dashboard may seem overly complex, but on the contrary it is extremely easy to use once you get used to it. It typically takes me five minutes to review the dashboard. Here's how to accomplish that:

1. Bring up http:// stockcharts.com for indicators except #6, which is obtained separately at http://www.aaii.com/ sentimentsurvey/.

2. For each indicator key in the respective ticker symbol. They are in order:

    $NYA50R;$COMPQ;$NYHL;$BPNYA`$SPX`$NASI

3. Follow the instructions on pages 126-131 to get the exact parameters you need.

4. You can keep the first stockcharts screen up after you finish viewing it and just key in the next symbol and change any parameters as necessary. After a short time, you'll be able to do this very fast.

5. Remember that #3, #4 and #6 need to be changed to "0," if six months have passed without a change in signal. On the exact day six months later change the value to "0". Of course, if the indicator gave another signal in the same direction as the original signal just extend the time forward another six months.

6. Keep your Dashboard on a spreadsheet or on graph paper with the indicators numbered on the left side and the dates across the top. This way you can easily tally the composite score for each day when there is a change. Enter a +1, -1 or 0 when there is a signal change. Alternatively, go to my blog on my website, www.buydonthold.com, to see the Dashboard there.

7. You may want to copy page 132 to keep handy for ready-reference.

Endnotes

1   Stovall, Sam. "Cyclical Six." *Standard & Poor's The Outlook*, November 18, 2009, p. 1.

6

Using Relative Strength Analysis to Determine Where to Invest

"Never follow the crowd."
Bernard Baruch, financier

"I can calculate the motions of the heavenly bodies but not the movements of the stock market."
Isaac Newton, scientist

The Basic Premise of Relative Strength Analysis

Relative strength analysis (RSA) is one approach that has been thoroughly tested over decades by academicians and used profitably by money managers, traders, and investors. The logic behind RSA is that the top performing stocks stay strong for weeks or months at a time and therefore provide investors with a significant money making opportunity. The main thesis of RSA is that the highest-ranked stocks based on price performance over a specific time frame compared to all others in a particular index (for example, S&P 500 Index or all

NYSE stocks) should be bought and held until they fall below a pre-determined relative strength ranking. At that point they should be sold and replaced by the top-ranked stocks.

Studies have determined that buying the weakest stocks instead of the strongest ones is a no-win proposition. In other words, the smart strategy is to buy stocks as they are making higher highs or in a solid uptrend. Investors often do the opposite, and buy stocks that have been beaten down, expecting them to rebound and skyrocket. This hope does not pan out in reality. Everyone wants a bargain and no one wants to pay up to buy anything, but when you are investing in the stock market, that is what turns out to be a profitable strategy. Bargain-basement shopping may work when you're buying clothes cheaply, but it characteristically does not work well in the stock market. Stay away from the losers, since they usually continue to be losers.

RSA involves ranking a specific group or universe of stocks, ETFs, or other investment vehicles on the basis of price performance, compared to each other over a specific time frame, such as 4 weeks, 12 weeks, 3 months, 6 months, or 12 months, and then buying a handful of the strongest ones. The ranking from best performing to worst performing is measured by the percentage increase in price from the beginning date of the selected measurement period to the ending date of that selected period. The stocks with the highest percentage change will be at the top of the list. One way of showing the results, in addition to using percentages, is to use percentile rankings. For example, with a 100-stock universe the strongest performing stock will be ranked 99 and the weakest will be ranked 1. Studies have shown that buying stocks based on either a very short ranking period such as a month or less or a long ranking period beyond 12 months doesn't work very well in producing profitable investing results. That is the reason I have opted to use a 6-month period as the most viable. When any of the top-ranked ETFs drop to a lower pre-determined rank, they are replaced with the highest-ranking non-duplicated candidates.

William O'Neil, publisher of *Investors Business Daily,* recommends that stocks be bought when they have high price momentum. His newspaper ranks all the stocks each day on relative price strength. Not everyone agrees that relative strength adds value to the stock selection process. For example, Burton Malkiel, Professor of Economics at Princeton, puts forth the view that any benefits of using relative strength are negated by increased transaction costs in buying and selling stock positions. Another argument against relative strength investing is that it is a tax-inefficient strategy since there are mostly short-term gains, which are taxed at a higher rate than long-term gains for positions held beyond one year. You have to weigh these arguments against the consistent returns shown by using the RSA to determine whether the results warrant its use. I suggest that you should not make investment decisions based solely on tax consequences, unless your investment is approaching a holding period of 12 months, which has a preferential capital gains rate. As far as transaction costs are concerned, that is no longer an issue because many discount brokers offer commissions below $10 a trade.

Relative Price Strength Test in 1969 and 1970

My first experience with RSA occurred in 1969 and 1970, when I was researching the topic in academic journals and investment books for my MBA thesis, titled "Statistical Evaluation of the Relative Strength Concept of Common Stock Selection." I read Robert Levy's book *The Relative Strength Concept of Common Stock Price Forecasting* (published in 1968), which spurred me on to investigate the subject in detail. He found that using certain filter rules based on relative strength criteria beat buy-and-hold when transaction costs were taken into account. This was contrary to the findings of academia who believed in the random-walk hypothesis that future stock performance could not be predicted using past data. They thought that stock prices have no memory and that using charts or other financial data was totally fruitless. They felt that an individual or a monkey throwing darts at *The Wall Street Journal* to select stocks would perform as well as any investment advisory service.

After renting a large electronic calculator, I set up four specific relative strength filter rules and meticulously analyzed the relative strength rankings of stocks over a fixed time frame that were ranked by Facts, Inc., in their weekly hard-copy report. I tested these strategies over a set time frame. Keep in mind that back then the PC, software, and the Internet were not available to me for back-testing purposes. My conclusion was that a few of the filters based on specific relative strength rankings did outperform buy-and-hold. Of course, that was not an in-depth test, but I continued to keep abreast of the subject. Since then I have found specific software and free Web sites (which will be provided later in this chapter) that provide relative price strength rankings of ETFs and stocks (only with software) over varying time frames with the click of a mouse. Now you can take advantage of this capability to build a viable investing approach.

Relative Strength Studies by Colby, O'Shaughnessy, and Kirkpatrick

The investment literature is replete with research indicating that using an RSA filter for selecting investments works well and consistently over time. In the past few decades, a number of books and studies have confirmed that RSA is an excellent way to build a portfolio that provides a better return than buy-and-hold with less risk. That is always the preferred combination of factors from any investor's perspective.

Robert W. Colby, CMT, a long-time market researcher and senior investment strategist at TradingEducation.com, as well as author of the exhaustive 820-page *Encyclopedia of Technical Market Indicators, Second Edition* (2003), found over many decades encompassing bull and bear market cycles that "relative strength" beats all other stock selection criteria.[1] He points out that the *Value Line Investment Survey* uses a relative strength measurement in its analysis and that their top-ranked stocks beat the Standard & Poor's 500 Index by 4.5 to 1 over a 15-year test period.

Colby simulated results by buying the top 10 ETFs weekly from a list of 235 (120 ETFs were used in his earlier 2004 work and expanded over time) and ranking them on a percentile basis from high to low. From August 20, 2004, to September 18, 2009, his simulated results produced a 115% price gain compared to a –3% loss for the S&P 500 Index.[2] Each week he ranked all the ETFs based on their price performance over the preceding six months and sold those that dropped off the Top 10 list, and bought the strongest ones not currently owned so that he had a portfolio of 10. Colby mentions on his Web site, www.robertwcolby.com, that "this Top 10 List is a research study and is not investment advice." Each week his Web site lists the top ETFs. Keep in mind that simulated results do not represent actual trading or take commissions or taxes into account.

During his earlier tests from August 6, 2004, to May 19, 2006, he found that a few ETFs were strong for extended time frames and remained in the Top 10. Here are a few examples:

Emerging Markets 50 BLDRS (33 weeks); iShares Brazil (55 weeks); and iShares S&P Latin American 40 (88 weeks). Colby's relative strength strategy also had good results when expanding to the top 20 and top 30 ETFs; however, he found that it worked best with the top 10. Some ETFs remain in the top category for weeks or months, but not for over a year, so you shouldn't expect to capture long-term capital gains beyond a year with this strategy.

Author James O'Shaughnessy (founder and chairman of the O'Shaughnessy Funds), in his first book, *What Works on Wall Street* (1994), and revised editions (1996 and 2005), studied relative strength analysis and concluded that buying stocks with high relative strength combined with a low price-to-sales ratio outperformed buy-and-hold over 45 years. In essence, he commented that relative strength was the only single growth variable which had the best performance compared to many other measures.

More recent work by Charles D. Kirkpatrick II, CMT, author of *Invest by Knowing What Stocks to Buy and What Stocks to Sell* (FT Press, 2009), confirmed the value of relative strength. He flatly states in his book: "The most reliable technique for selecting stocks is relative price strength." He found that the top-ranked relative strength stocks beat the indexes by 7.7 times to 1 over a 25-year period.

Kirkpatrick measured relative price strength over a six-month period and found that the best overall performance results occurred over the following three months to a year. He back-tested his strategy from 1998 to 2006, evaluating more than 8,073 stocks with 290,594 weekly observations. He tested three relative strength strategies, including relative price strength, in which stocks were ranked against each other on a scale of 99 to 1 (strongest to weakest), as well as the price-to-sales ratio. He discovered that the highest ranked stocks based on price performance normally continue to increase in price for a period of up to one year, thus providing investors with profitable results. Stocks were sold when their rank dropped to a predetermined level. Combining relative strength with the price-to-sales ratio produced excellent results.

Kirkpatrick found that using the 90th percentile ranking as the cutoff for investing in the best candidates produced too many viable stocks in some of his tests, so he increased the filter to the 97th percentile (97 ranking) or even higher to be more selective. He sold any stocks in the portfolio when their ranking dropped to 52, and replaced them with the top ranking stocks. Furthermore, he found that relative price strength criteria performed well whether in bull or bear markets. However, he adjusted his sell ranking to 37 in bear markets.

Relative Strength Investing with ETFs— A Great Combination

In your investing plan, ETFs should be used as the vehicle of choice for the reasons previously discussed in Chapter 4, "Exchange-Traded Funds—The Most Suitable Investment Vehicles." That chapter provides a listing of the specific ETFs for your investing plan, as well as the percent allocation among the asset classes dependent on your risk tolerance—conservative, moderate, aggressive, or very aggressive. You can fine-tune any of the percentage allocations in specific ETFs to better suit your needs. You shouldn't necessarily be concerned that you are a few percentage points off, if you are on the borderline of conservative/moderate or moderate/aggressive. Just select an overall allocation that you are comfortable with, and remember that you can always adjust the plan to work better after your real-time experience.

Therefore, your next step is to rank your selected ETF universe based on its most recent six-month price performance to determine which ETFs are the most attractive purchase candidates. This time frame was selected instead of a shorter or longer time frame because a number of research studies found that the six-month time frame offered reliable results over time. Of course, I could have used a weighted average approach, for example, the six-month period with 75% weighting, the three-month period with 15% weighting, and the one-week period with 10% weighting. However, I wanted to not only make the process as simple as possible for you to follow, but also make sure that the ranking information was available from free Web sites.

Always Check the ETF's Chart Before Purchase

Make sure before you buy any ETF that you not only review its component investments, but look at a two-year price chart with a 50-dma and MACD indicator, to see whether it is in an uptrend confirmed by the MACD. Why do that? The reason is simple. Although an ETF may be highly ranked, it may not be in an uptrend because the entire stock market may be starting to drop as it did from October 2007 through March 2009. During that time frame, almost 100% of all regular ETFs (not inverse ones) had *negative* price performance. Those with the top relative strength rankings were all *dropping* in price, but less than the other ETFs. Bringing up a chart will instantly give you a picture of the trend. Moreover, your prior weekly review of the "Stock Market Dashboard" would have warned you well in advance that the market was not a "buy" at the moment. Remember, the dashboard must have given a "buy" signal before you consider purchasing any ETF.

A *Limited ETF Investing Universe*

For the sake of simplicity, I recommend that your ETF investing universe be limited to 66 in total from the following diverse categories (as mentioned in Chapter 4):

- **Morningstar style box**—There are 9 ETFs, including small-, mid-, and large-cap with either a value or growth focus or a blending of the two.
- **SPDR sectors**—There are 9 different sector ETFs.
- **International**—There are 32 separate country ETFs, including two multicountry ones (EEM and EFA).
- **Fixed income**—There are 10 different bond ETFs such as investment grade, treasury, long- and short-term bonds, and municipals.
- **Specialty**—There are 6 ETFs, including oil, gold, silver, solar energy, REIT, and agriculture.

Each of the five ETF categories will be ranked separately and then combined as one universe with the benchmark and inverse funds so that you can get the top-down picture of the top-ranked ETFs, irrespective of category. Among the benchmarks included in our universe are SPY (Standard & Poor's 500), QQQQ (NASDAQ

100), and VTI (Wilshire 5000 index represented by the Vanguard Total Stock Market ETF). Five inverse ETFs were also included. When you notice that bonds, gold, and the inverse ETFs start ascending the table with higher and higher rankings, that will be an *early warning signal* that a current uptrend is waning, if you have not already been forewarned by the dashboard.

ETF Selection Strategy #1 Category

After you rank the ETFs separately by each category and then as a combined universe as illustrated in the next section, you'll need to select ETFs to buy. Based on your investor profile, I suggest selecting the top two to four ranked ETFs in each of three categories—style, sector, and fixed income—and buy one or two ETFs from the specialty category. Because there are 34 international ETFs, I suggest that you *invest in the top 4 to 6 countries.* In total, I recommend a total of 15 ETFs for each investor profile.

ETF Selection Strategy #2 Entire Universe

Instead of investing by category as mentioned in strategy #1, the *other choice is to select the top 15 ETFs from the entire composite universe,* since the cream will rise to the top. This may result in a concentration of international ETFs, for example, when they are all the strongest performers. You will have to decide whether this approach is too risky for you or whether you can be disciplined enough to monitor the ETFs each week, and replace them as necessary when they fall in ranking to 34th or below. This strategy will most likely produce higher returns than strategy #1, but it will also have a higher risk and volatility. *Investing 100% in international ETFs or in all equity ETFs should be considered by only very aggressive disciplined investors.* The reason is simple. That particular portfolio would be the most risky and volatile of all in our universe. For example, a few of the international funds dropped 25% a few times in the past year, before rallying strongly, and surging ahead.

Be very careful when selecting the top-ranked ETFs after a buy signal is given, because the strongest ETFs at a market bottom will invariably be the inverse funds and bonds. *You want to avoid those entirely.* Focus your attention on the regular equity ETFs in these categories: style, sectors, and countries. Carefully monitor the weekly rankings after a market bottom has been reached as the market starts to rebound. Initially, look for those ETFs that also have a strong 4-week and 26-week (6-month) ranking to give you an idea as to which ones are increasing the fastest since the positive trend change. At the turning point after a bottom has been reached, you have to select from the universe ETFs that have the most potential. Typically those are the ones that are near the top of the rankings even though they may have negative performance numbers. Remember do not buy the inverse funds or bonds at the market bottom.

WARNING: If you invest 100% in international ETFs, put on your seat belt and wear a helmet because the roller coaster ride will have many ups and downs, twists, and turns. Always use stops to protect your principal.

When to Sell ETFs That Fall in the Ranking

After you have your 15-ETF portfolio, each week you can monitor their latest week's *six-month performance ranking* to determine whether any ETF has dropped below half of its ETF ranking positions. At that point, that ETF should be sold and the highest-ranked non-duplicated ETF purchased with the proceeds of the sale to replace it. Thus, if an ETF that you are holding drops to the following ranking positions in its category, it should be sold:

- 5th-ranked position or lower for the Morningstar style (9 ETFs)
- 5th-ranked position or lower for the SPDR sectors (9 ETFs)
- 6th-ranked position or lower for the fixed income (10 ETFs)
- 17th-ranked position or lower for the international ETFs (32 ETFs)
- 4th-ranked position or lower for specialty ETFs (6 ETFs)

Using www.etfscreen.com to Rank ETFs

Now that you know how many ETFs to invest in and when they should be bought and sold, you need to find a source of relative strength data. Therefore, let's review two free Web sites that you can use to obtain the price performance and relative strength rankings of your ETF universe. The first site is www.etfscreen.com. It offers ETF price performance and relative strength ranking as of the market's closing price each day by family, style, country, and industry or sector. And it ranks them from top to bottom over varying time frames by percentage price change—daily, weekly, monthly, quarterly, biannually, and yearly.

This site contains the information you need in one place, provides both a raw percentage change in price and a relative strength ranking (on a scale of 99 to 1) on separate matrixes, provides a chart of any ETF, includes a price comparison chart of up to nine ETFs at once, includes a correlation matrix comparing ETFs, and provides customized ETF lists that can be saved as favorites.

Basic Information Provided

Before you review this information-packed Web site, I suggest that you become familiar with it by going online. Click the buttons on the left side of the screen and across the top of the screen, and then click the up and down arrows. One terrific feature of this Web site is the capability to create your own custom ETF list, instead of using only the current ETF categories. As you recall, we also need to place all the recommended ETFs in one composite list, as well as separate ones by asset category. That is easy to accomplish on this site, as you shall see.

This site provides the six-month percentage price change measurement and a *weighted average* relative strength ranking (RSf values), which works out to approximately a six-month time horizon. The

RSf tables shown are for the past 13 weeks; however, the columns are not sortable. That would have been a nice feature since you could see which ETF was strong 13 weeks ago and then see its rankings over the more current 12 weeks, as the other columns' data would have been automatically resorted.

By clicking the Correlation Data box on the left side of the screen, and then Comparison Charting at the bottom of the new page, you are provided with a matrix showing the correlation of one ETF to another and a chart in multicolors showing each ETF's price performance over the past six months compared to a maximum of nine ETFs. Refer to our initial discussion on risk in Chapter 2, "Understanding the Concept of Risk," where correlation was explained. You will recall that the correlation coefficient ranges between -1 and $+1$. When you bring up this matrix, you can easily see which ETFs are strongly or weakly correlated to each other. When you are building an ETF portfolio, it is advantageous to have ETFs that are weakly correlated to provide diversification.

Web Site Style and Market Segment Views

This Web site sorts the 760-plus ETF universe (as of September 18, 2009) into the categories shown next. The bolded items are the categories we will use as our ETF universe.

Styles

- **Morningstar**
- S&P/Barra
- Russell
- Dow Jones
- Vanguard

Market Segments

- **U.S. Broad Mkt** (only to obtain the specialty funds and benchmarks)
- All Sector ETFs

- Dow Jones Sectors
- **Select Sector SPDRs**
- Merrill Lynch HOLDRS
- **International—Country**
- International—Regional
- International—Misc.
- Natural Resources
- **Fixed Income**
- Dividend Funds
- Currencies

Table 6.1a, for example, is a basic ETF Performance (measuring price performance) matrix focusing only on the Morningstar Style ETFs. The table shows each ETF's name, ticker symbol, relative strength rating (on a scale of 99 to 1) over approximately the past six months, and percent change in price of each ETF for the six different periods shown, which include today, past five days, one month, three months, six months, and one year. You can sort each of these columns in ascending or descending order by clicking on the up or down arrow at the top of each column. Your focus should be on the strongest ETFs at the top of the list using the column labeled "6 Mths." Looking at the actual data on the Web site, one can see that the color dark blue is used for the strongest price gainers and red is used to highlight the weakest performers.

Table 6.1b is for the same universe but the data is shown as relative strength percentile rankings. This table ranks the prior table's ETFs on a ranking basis from 99 (strongest performer) to 1 (weakest performer), and provides an easy way to see the change in weekly ranking, especially with the color coding on the Web site. This table shows the ETF ranking for the current and past 12 weeks so you can see the trend in ranking scores. A 99 ranking means than an ETF has performed better than 99% of its universe.

TABLE 6.1a   Morningstar Style Box ETF Performance (As of the Close September 18, 2009); Percent Change in Price over Selected Time Periods

Name ∧v	Symbol ∧v	RSf ∧v	1 Day ∧v	5 Days ∧v	1 Mth ∧v	3 Mths ∧v	6 Mths ∧v	1 Year ∧v
iShares Morningstar Small Value Index Fund	JKL	82.06	0.11	−4.68	13.39	33.52	76.57	−7.28
iShares Morningstar Mid Value Index Fund	JKI	71.75	0.14	4.12	11.33	28.46	65.74	−6.84
iShares Morningstar Small Core Index Fund	JKJ	69.48	0.36	3.63	11.49	23.56	64.34	−7.9
iShares Morningstar Mid Core Index Fund	JKG	61.98	0.41	3.17	10.12	23.04	54.44	−7.25
iShares Morningstar Small Growth	JKK	52.21	0.16	3.13	9.76	16.64	50.75	−9.37
iShares Morningstar Mid Growth Index Fund	JKH	49.93	0.15	2.73	9.03	17.63	44.1	−10.37
iShares Morningstar Large Growth Index Fund	JKE	43.51	−0.02	1.51	7.35	13.16	35.82	−6.42
iShares Morningstar Large Core Index Fund	JKD	38.69	0.44	2.24	6.74	16.11	40.43	−10.05
iShares Morningstar Large Value Index Fund	JKF	31.99	0.19	2.57	6.21	15.96	34.37	−11.11

Reprinted with permission of www.etfscreen.com

CHAPTER 6 • USING RELATIVE STRENGTH ANALYSIS

TABLE 6.1b Relative Strength Percentile Ranking of Morningstar Style Box ETFs; Viewing Weekly Periods

Symbol	09/18	09/11	09/03	08/27	08/20	08/13	08/06	07/30	07/23	07/16	07/09	07/01	06/24
JKL	82	78	77	85	79	78	72	62	56	53	45	57	41
JKI	71	69	73	78	71	70	62	59	51	46	37	48	42
JKJ	69	66	62	71	68	68	62	63	60	59	49	60	50
JKG	61	57	56	60	63	62	59	52	49	44	41	44	42
JKK	52	53	50	55	57	56	54	66	68	68	60	65	57
JKH	49	46	42	41	48	48	36	45	46	37	36	37	36
JKD	38	34	37	38	38	36	34	41	45	49	47	39	41
JKE	43	43	45	43	44	44	45	54	65	62	56	49	56
JKF	31	26	30	37	35	29	25	23	21	25	22	21	20

Reprinted with permission of www.etfscreen.com

When you click the ETF name on the actual Web site (Table 6.1a in our example) or the ticker symbol (Table 6.1b in our example), a high-quality candlestick chart with a 50- and 200-dma with the daily transaction volume is shown on the screen. The chart time frame can be adjusted by changing the Chart Option choice located below the chart. And you can compare this fund to any other by keying in their ticker symbols in the box under Compare Multi-Fund Performance.

For your review, I have included the following eight tables (as of the closing prices of September 18, 2009) obtained from the Web site to show examples of our recommended asset categories:

- Table 6.1a, Morningstar Style Box ETF Performance
- Table 6.1b, Relative Strength Percentile Ranking of Morningstar Style Box ETFs
- Table 6.2a, Select Sector SPDRs Performance
- Table 6.2b, Relative Strength Percentile Ranking of Select Sector SPDRs
- Table 6.3a, International—Country ETF Performance
- Table 6.3b, Relative Strength Percentile Ranking of Country ETFs
- Table 6.4a, Fixed Income ETF Performance
- Table 6.4b, Relative Strength Percentile Ranking of Fixed Income ETFs

Morningstar Style Box

As you can see in Table 6.1a, the strongest two performers over the past six months were small- and mid-cap value, up 76.57% and 65.74%, respectively. They have also maintained their top performance positions over the past three months, one month, and five days. Their relative strength ranking was 82.06 and 71.75, respectively, as shown in the RSf column. Table 6.1b shows these rankings as well, for the week ending September 18, 2009. We can see on that table that beginning with August 6, both of these ETFs started leading the others, and their performance has remained strong since then.

SPDRs Select Sectors

As you can see in Table 6.2a, the strongest two performers over the past six months were the financial and industrial sectors, up 87.53% and 57.19%, respectively. They have also maintained their top performance positions almost perfectly over the past three months. Table 6.2b shows the relative strength rankings, for the week ending September 18 and prior weeks. By viewing this table, you can easily ascertain which ETFs are improving or deteriorating on a relative basis to each other over the past six months.

The financial and industrial sector relative strength ranking for the most recent week was 64.93 and 50.74, respectively, as shown in the RSf column of Table 6.2a and of course Table 6.2b. In the latter table, the industrial's relative strength ranking has dropped to fifth out of nine, so this sector may be starting to give up its top-two ranking soon.

We can see that beginning with August 20, the financials started leading the others and their performance has remained strong, except for the week of September 11, when it dropped to second place.

Interestingly, consumer discretionary, energy, and utilities haven't changed that much in ranking from 6/24 to 9/18. Financial, materials, and industrials have improved. The three top-ranked ETFs on this matrix are financial, materials, and consumer discretionary. But their rankings are only 64, 58, and 56, respectively. So even though they are the three top sectors, their relative strength is not that strong compared to the highest ranked ETFs at 99 (not on this table). Comparing these sector funds with the International—Country ETFs in the upcoming discussion of Tables 6.3a and 6.3b, we find that their top performers are ranked 90 and higher. Therefore, you know that the Select Sector SPDRs are not leading the ETF parade.

TABLE 6.2a Select Sector SPDRs Performance (As of the Close September 18, 2009); Percent Change in Price over Selected Time Periods

Name ∧	Symbol ∧	RSf ∧	1 Day ∧	5 Days ∧	1 Mth ∧	3 Mths ∧	6 Mths ∧	1 Year ∧
Select Sector SPDR Fund—Financial	XLF	64.93	-0.15	4.52	9.18	26.14	87.53	-21.05
Select Sector SPDR Fund—Industrial	XLI	50.74	-0.57	3.05	11.47	22.31	57.19	-14.3
Select Sector SPDR Fund—Materials	XLB	58.9	-0.05	4.39	9.07	23.29	52.78	-9.66
Select Sector SPDR Fund—Consumer Discretionary	XLY	56.63	0.36	2.99	8.95	20.58	50.99	-5.49
SPDR S&P 500	SPY	42.57	0.06	2.35	7.27	16.5	40.57	-8.29
Select Sector SPDR Fund—Technology	XLK	55.69	0.61	1.34	7.09	15.71	40.04	2.27
Select Sector SPDR Fund—Energy Select Sector	XLE	26.51	-0.35	3.41	9.8	12.63	29.55	-16.02
Select Sector SPDR Fund—Consumer Staples	XLP	27.58	1.31	0.99	5.06	11.76	25.31	-6.6
Select Sector SPDR Fund—Health Care	XLV	26.91	-0.43	-0.12	2.47	10.76	23.28	-6.4
Select Sector SPDR Fund—Utilities	XLU	23.96	0.46	3.62	3.72	9.16	19.64	-8.43

Reprinted with permission of www.etfscreen.com

TABLE 6.2b Relative Strength Percentile Ranking of Select Sector SPDRs; Viewing Weekly Periods

Symbol	09/18	09/11	09/03	08/27	08/20	08/13	08/06	07/30	07/23	07/16	07/09	07/01	06/24
XLF	64	54	80	78	80	63	46	28	24	22	30	24	20
XLB	58	52	60	53	54	67	67	55	61	37	33	32	29
XLY	56	54	57	70	70	72	63	63	64	64	54	58	55
XLK	55	61	59	61	67	67	69	69	79	79	73	69	73
XLI	50	40	35	40	34	33	24	20	19	24	20	22	21
SPY	42	37	41	44	42	42	38	38	41	36	38	36	38
XLP	27	26	27	31	25	27	33	40	42	54	56	48	52
XLV	26	35	37	40	32	25	30	50	43	46	57	49	56
XLE	26	20	17	16	16	15	15	18	25	23	17	15	14
XLU	23	19	23	23	27	21	22	26	34	36	31	33	35

Reprinted with permission of www.etfscreen.com

Back-Test of SPDR Relative Strength

The use of the SPDR momentum strategy presented previously has historical precedence. As reported on www.seekingalpha.com, a back-tested study was performed on the nine Select Sector SPDRs from January 1999 to May 2008.[3] In the first month, $10,000 was invested in the strongest performing SPDR over the previous six-month period. For each month thereafter, the existing funds were invested in the strongest single SPDR over the past six-month period. The existing SPDR was held only when it was number "1" in the ranking; otherwise, it was sold and replaced by the best performing one. At the end of the test period, the sector momentum strategy aggregated to about $26,000 in value compared to about $11,500 for buy-and-holding the S&P 500 Index. Interestingly, over the 107-month period the Energy Select SPDR was the leading fund in 39 months, resulting in a large portion of the return.

International—Country ETFs

As you can see by looking at Tables 6.3a and 6.3b, the international ETFs were sizzling, and racked up huge gains, with four ETFs showing gains of over 100% in just six months. Only Indonesia and Turkey have retained their dominant strength over the past six months, with rankings of 99 each in the most current week. International ETFs have high volatility and can drop as fast or faster than they rise, which was the case in 2008. So be very careful with these ETFs.

TABLE 6.3a International—Country ETF Performance (Only a Portion of Countries Shown); Percent Change in Price over Selected Time Periods

Name ᴧⱽ	Symbol ᴧⱽ	RSf ᴧⱽ	1 Day ᴧⱽ	5 Days ᴧⱽ	1 Mth ᴧⱽ	3 Mths ᴧⱽ	6 Mths ᴧⱽ	1 Year ᴧⱽ
Market Vectors Indonesia ETF	IDX	99.33	-0.03	3.98	12.53	37.2	144.01	n/a
iShares MSCI Turkey Invest Mkt Index	TUR	99.06	0.59	2.1	3.45	38.13	128.8	27.78
iPath MSCI India ETN	INP	95.85	0.44	3.16	13.54	17.94	106.5	19.23
WisdomTree India Earnings	EPI	96.25	1.08	3.99	13.07	19.16	104.21	22.21
iShares MSCI Austria Index Fund	EWO	94.38	-0.6	2.79	15.29	38.96	90.62	-3.41
PowerShares India	PIN	91.7	1.16	3.32	12.78	14.65	89.19	18.48
iShares MSCI Singapore Index Fund	EWS	89.16	-0.83	-0.83	7.01	20.88	85.7	11.02
Market Vectors Russia ETF Trust	RSX	92.24	1.35	4.72	20.8	26.98	84.96	-3.65
iShares MSCI Thailand Invest Mkt Index	THD	95.72	1.2	1.87	14.78	24.9	84.3	24.01
iShares MSCI South Korea Index Fund	EWY	95.18	0.52	4.37	15.06	35.43	75.75	13.72
PowerShares Golden Dragon Halter USX China Portfolio	PGJ	85.01	-0.54	2.71	7.77	14.49	74.93	15.82
iShares MSCI Spain Index Fund	EWP	88.35	0.82	4.21	12.59	30.84	74.11	15.86

Reprinted with permission of www.etfscreen.com

TABLE 6.3b Relative Strength Percentile Ranking of Country ETFs

Symbol	09/18	09/11	09/03	08/27	08/20	08/13	08/06	07/30	07/23	07/16	07/09	07/01	06/24
IDX	99	99	98	99	99	99	99	99	99	98	99	99	99
TUR	99	99	99	98	98	98	98	98	98	97	97	96	96
EPI	96	95	94	95	93	97	98	98	98	98	98	98	98
EWZ	95	94	93	91	96	94	94	95	94	93	92	94	92
INP	95	96	94	96	90	96	98	97	98	98	97	99	98
THD	95	97	96	95	95	95	96	96	96	97	98	97	97
EWY	95	96	97	97	95	87	88	91	88	80	88	74	59
EWD	94	95	95	95	94	93	90	92	90	90	80	88	65
EWO	94	95	94	94	91	85	78	76	73	73	51	55	40
BRF	94	92	92	91	96	n/a	n/a	n/a	n/a	n/a	n/a	n/a	n/a
EWA	93	96	95	92	92	94	89	88	82	83	65	69	64
EZA	92	93	95	90	90	90	91	90	97	95	94	93	91
RSX	92	86	77	71	84	80	87	92	90	56	53	84	59
PIN	91	88	88	89	83	94	95	96	96	97	96	98	98
EWT	90	90	89	54	71	83	82	89	93	94	95	89	88
EWS	89	93	94	92	90	92	93	96	93	94	94	94	88
GXC	88	86	87	90	95	96	97	98	97	96	97	96	96
EWP	88	92	92	93	90	92	90	91	86	87	77	85	71

Reprinted with permission of www.etfscreen.com

Fixed Income ETFs

Compared to the performance of the international country ETFs, the fixed income ETFs' performance appear to be comatose. But that is incorrectly comparing apples to oranges. Fixed income investments are useful as an alternative asset class, and they typically counterbalance equity investments, and therefore usually act defensively in bear markets. For example, Barclays Capital U.S. Aggregate Bond Index rose in the bear market years of 2000–2002, as well as 2008, by 11.63%, 8.44%, 10.26%, and 5.24%, respectively in each year. Conservative investors typically have the highest percentage of bonds in their portfolios.

For some reason, the S&P 500 Index appears in Table 6.4a, possibly for comparative reasons, because it contains no bonds. As this table indicates, the top-performing bonds over our six-month time horizon were SPDR Barclays High Yield Bond, and an iShares iBoxx $ High Yield Bond at a 39.9% and 33.62% return, respectively. As you can see, four out of the top six bonds were in the high-yield category. In your ETF portfolio you do not want to duplicate similar investments, so you can select JNK and LWC. You should understand that high-yield bonds have had a roller coaster ride over the past year and are volatile bonds compared to other categories. You would also want to check out LWC's portfolio on www.morningstar.com and the fund's Web site to see what it holds, to make sure that it does not contain any high-yield bonds. By the way, www.marketwatch.com (ETF tab) is a site that contains a large amount of data on all ETFs regarding their objective, holdings, performance, and so forth. Become familiar with this site as an ETF investor. *Before you invest in any ETF, as mentioned earlier, you should review its components and other details. If you do not feel comfortable with any ETF, then do not include it in your investing universe. Just substitute another one.*

TABLE 6.4a Fixed Income ETF Performance (As of the Close September 18, 2009); Percent Change in Price over Selected Time Periods

Name ⌄	Symbol ⌄	RSf ⌄	1 Day ⌄	5 Days ⌄	1 Mth ⌄	3 Mths ⌄	6 Mths ⌄	1 Year ⌄
SPDR S&P 500	SPY	42.57	0.06	2.35	7.27	16.5	40.57	-8.29
SPDR Barclays High Yield Bond	JNK	66.4	0.13	2.81	6.01	12.26	39.9	10.58
iShares iBoxx $ High Yield Corporate Bond Fund	HYG	55.56	-0.28	2.02	5.95	12.52	33.62	9.13
PowerShares High Yield Corporate Bond Portfolio	PHB	40.16	-0.51	1.43	5.17	9.1	26.78	-2.84
SPDR Barclays Capital Long Credit Bond	LWC	24.63	-0.11	-0.22	2.26	14.64	25.08	n/a
Market Vectors High-Yield Muni ETF	HYD	18.34	0.36	2.13	8.56	12.41	19.66	n/a
iShares iBoxx $ Invst Grd Cp Bd	LQD	38.96	-0.63	-0.4	2.35	7.78	15.12	23.48

Reprinted with permission of www.etfscreen.com

Interestingly, Table 6.4b shows that all the bonds shown have declined in relative strength from June 24, 2009, to the latest week. This makes sense because the stock market bottomed on March 9, 2009, and has had a spectacular run in a short time frame, leaving bonds in the dust.

Composite Rankings on Our Customized ETF List and Comparison Chart

Now that we have covered four of the five individual groupings of ETFs in your investment universe, except for the specialty funds and comparable benchmarks, let's see how to obtain all these items on separate performance and relative strength tables. To do so, open the www.etfscreen.com Web site and click on any ETF name or ticker symbol. This will automatically bring up a chart of the fund. Under the chart on the right side is a box with the words "compare multi-fund performance." All you have to do is type in the ticker symbols of the ETFs that I have provided in Appendix 6.1 at the end of this chapter. I suggest that you first type out this list in Word and then paste it in wherever you need it. When entering it on this Web site, make sure that you separate each symbol with a space and that you have a total of 74 ETFs. You can then save this site as a "favorite" with everything saved. There is a limit of 100 symbols that can be saved, but we are under that limit. And you can add or delete any new symbols that you'd like or create your own categories of ETFs and save them as separate favorites. Moreover, you can place each category of ETFs in a separate portfolio using this approach and save each one as a favorite. This approach provides a quick and easy way to check each category by just opening each favorite with the preselected ETFs.

TABLE 6.4b Relative Strength Percentile Ranking of Fixed Income ETFs; Viewing Weekly Periods

Symbol	09/18	09/11	09/03	08/27	08/20	08/13	08/06	07/30	07/23	07/16	07/09	07/01	06/24
SPY	42	37	41	44	42	42	38	38	41	36	38	36	38
JNK	66	66	63	62	65	66	83	78	76	80	90	88	92
HYG	55	57	51	51	51	56	77	75	74	77	85	88	85
PHB	40	35	34	34	33	36	58	53	47	48	73	72	70
LWC	24	24	63	51	53	50	61	52	28	49	56	24	33
HYD	18	16	14	13	13	14	23	19	18	33	40	19	20
LQD	38	43	49	43	48	50	70	67	68	81	91	86	92

Reprinted with permission of www.etfscreen.com

As you can see by viewing Tables 6.5a and 6.5b, the international ETFs overwhelmingly dominate the top six-month performance and relative strength rankings. Note that SPDR financials (XLF) is the sixth-ranked ETF. So even with a heart-throbbing six-month return of 87.53%, it was not at the top of our universe. It is quite interesting to see ICF, a real estate ETF, in third place, up 97.38% for the period, in light of the devastation in the real estate market over the past year. And ICF has had strong recent performance as well in the three-month, one-month, and five-day period, even with continued negative news about real estate. That's why it pays to ignore the fundamental and headline news on Wall Street, as well as the economic forecasts. Instead, just focus on the price movement of individual ETFs to see which ones are leading the market higher. Lastly, small-cap value ETF (JKL) did very well in the tenth position at 76.57%.

A quick look at Table 6.5b indicates that the Indonesia, India, and Austria ETFs are still powering ahead with a relative strength ranking above 90, while the three noncountry ETFs just mentioned are showing a weakening ranking trend of 82, 76, and 65. Also, note that every ETF ranked 83 or higher on this table is an international one. The strongest ETFs on this table as of September 18, 2009, were Indonesia, Turkey, and Brazil. Always wait for the appropriate dashboard buy signal, check the price chart, and consider putting in a stop-loss order when dealing with all ETFs, especially international ones. However, you may need to use a stop-loss order of 15% to 25% (if you can stomach the ride) from your purchase price of each country ETF because of potential volatility caused by a general market drop or unexpected economic or financial news from that particular country.

TABLE 6.5a   ETF Composite Performance Universe (As of September 18, 2009)

Name ^v	Symbol ^v	RSf ^v	1 Day ^v	5 Days ^v	1 Mth ^v	3 Mths ^v	6 Mths ^v	1 Year ^v
Market Vectors Indonesia ETF	IDX	99.33	-0.03	3.98	12.53	37.2	144.01	n/a
iShares MSCI Turkey Invest Mkt Index	TUR	99.06	0.59	2.1	3.45	38.13	128.8	27.78
iShares Cohen & Steers Realty Majors Index Fund	ICF	76.31	0.02	9.55	21.18	42.66	97.38	-32.23
iShares MSCI Austria Index Fund	EWO	94.38	-0.6	2.79	15.29	38.96	90.62	-3.41
PowerShares India	PIN	91.7	1.16	3.32	12.78	14.65	89.19	18.48
Select Sector SPDR Fund—Financial	XLF	64.93	-0.15	4.52	9.18	26.14	87.53	-21.05
iShares MSCI Singapore Index Fund	EWS	89.16	-0.83	-0.83	7.01	20.88	85.7	11.02
Market Vectors Russia ETF Trust	RSX	92.24	1.35	4.72	20.8	26.98	84.96	-3.65
iShares MSCI Thailand Invest Mkt Index	THD	95.72	1.2	1.87	14.78	24.9	84.3	24.01
iShares MSCI Morningstar Small Value Index Fund	JKL	82.06	0.11	4.68	13.39	33.52	76.57	-7.28
iShares MSCI South Korea Index Fund	EWY	95.18	0.52	4.37	15.06	35.43	75.75	13.72
iShares MSCI Spain Index Fund	EWP	88.35	0.82	4.21	12.59	30.84	74.11	15.86
iShares MSCI Sweden Index Fund	EWD	94.65	0.66	2.45	10.88	36.76	73.91	14.54
iShares MSCI Brazil Index Fund	EWZ	95.98	0.43	4.29	9.79	23.62	72.74	25.79
iShares MSCI Italy Index Fund	EWI	71.49	0.24	3.06	13.81	27.23	72.49	-3.58
iShares MSCI Australia Index Fund	EWA	93.84	0.09	2.89	12.73	31.56	72.11	14.07

Printed with permission of www.etfscreen.com

TABLE 6.5b Relative Strength Ranking of Composite Universe

Symbol	09/18	09/11	09/03	08/27	08/20	08/13	08/06	07/30	07/23	07/16	07/09	07/01	06/24
IDX	99	99	98	99	99	99	99	99	99	98	99	99	99
TUR	99	99	99	98	98	98	98	98	98	97	97	96	96
ICF	76	39	46	57	50	49	34	12	10	10	9	11	9
EWO	94	95	94	94	91	85	78	76	73	73	51	55	40
PIN	91	88	88	89	83	94	95	96	96	97	96	98	98
XLF	64	54	80	78	80	63	46	28	24	22	30	24	20
EWS	89	93	94	92	90	92	93	96	93	94	94	94	94
RSX	92	86	77	71	84	80	87	92	90	56	53	84	59
THD	95	97	96	95	95	95	96	96	96	97	98	97	97
JKL	82	78	77	85	79	78	72	62	56	53	45	57	41
EWY	95	96	97	97	95	87	88	91	88	80	88	74	59
EWP	88	92	92	93	90	92	90	91	86	87	77	85	71
EWD	94	95	95	95	94	93	90	92	90	90	80	88	65
EWZ	95	94	93	91	96	94	94	95	94	93	92	94	92
EWI	71	76	72	61	48	55	48	55	53	45	34	43	28
EWA	93	96	95	92	92	94	89	88	82	83	65	69	64
KWT	22	13	9	9	10	10	9	28	17	12	13	12	23
EWW	72	77	84	88	86	87	86	87	85	69	63	65	56

TABLE 6.5b Relative Strength Ranking of Composite Universe (continued)

Symbol	09/18	09/11	09/03	08/27	08/20	08/13	08/06	07/30	07/23	07/16	07/09	07/01	06/24
EWK	81	85	84	79	65	60	55	60	63	68	59	45	26
EWN	80	81	75	74	63	68	69	70	69	65	46	42	26
JKI	71	69	73	78	71	70	62	59	51	46	37	48	42
FXI	83	78	79	84	92	95	96	97	97	94	96	95	94
EEM	87	86	87	85	88	90	89	91	93	89	91	88	84
JKJ	69	66	62	71	68	68	62	63	60	59	49	60	50

Printed with permission of www.etfscreen.com

Scrolling down to the bottom of Table 6.5a (not shown due to space limitations), you should not be surprised that the ProShares inverse ETFs have the worst performance—because they fall as the market rises. The five shown in the full table are down 32% to 52% for the six-month period. And a number of the bond ETFs are poor performers. When you find these specific ETFs starting to move up in the table, be aware that the underlying market may be weakening. By the time they rise to the top, you should have been in cash for quite a while, based on the signals from the dashboard. Simply monitor these two tables every week and you will be tuned into the market's shenanigans. You don't need anyone's input on where the market is going or what to buy or sell. You have all the information right in front of you, coupled with the dashboard signals. You are in control of your portfolio and you know exactly what steps to take. Therefore, there is no need for concern or panic as you are monitoring the pulse of the market.

Using www.etftable.com to Rank ETFs

Another high-quality, full-featured, easy-to-use free Web site that provides ETF performance data over multiple time frames is www. etftable.com. Nathan Davis developed this color-coded ETF screener. According to Davis, this tool ranks ETFs by performance, relative strength, and trend indicators. It provides traders and investors with tools to filter ETFs by various technical analysis indicators, such as trend, performance, and volume. The goal of ETFtable.com is to allow users to create effective ETF trading strategies by providing the tools to choose the best ETFs for their goals and risk tolerance. I suggest that you go to the Web site and become familiar with its capabilities before going any farther in this section.

Now refer to Table 6.6a. This Web site's data provides intraday price changes with a time-delay, as well as the more typical one-day, one-week, four-week, three-month, and six-month percent price changes. In addition, there is a calculation showing the percentage amount (above or below) for various moving average crossovers. Each of the price performance and crossover columns is color-coded online to show the rank of that column (green is good, red is bad) for an ETF within the entire universe of ETFs.

SPDRs Select Sectors Example

Table 6.6a provides a look at the Select Sector SPDRs, as of the close October 5, 2009. If you click on the 6-Month header column, you will obtain the top-performing ETFs at the top of the table. One great feature is the availability of relative strength ranking data for each of the time frames. Go to the Relative Strength Rank view (top-right corner of the Web site) to bring up that view. You then just click on the 6-Month column to find the rankings in percentile format in both ascending and descending order. And you can sort any of the other columns on the table in ascending and descending order. You can see at a glance which ETFs are still strong over more recent time frames and which ones may be coming to the top over the next few months.

Look at Table 6.6b to see the relative strength of the Select Sector SPDRs. Viewing the table, you can see that XLF and XLI have the strongest RS for the six-month period, at 91 and 64, respectively. These ETFs have similar rankings for the three-month RS, but seem to be losing strength in the more recent periods. This information can forewarn you that future six-month readings may soon weaken over the next several weeks as well, so pay attention to this chart.

Another useful feature of this site is the ability to obtain a chart of any ETF supplied automatically from www.stockcharts.com. Just click on the ticker symbol and a chart will pop up to the right of the table. The price chart already includes the 50-dma and 200-dma, as well as the MACD, on the lower screen.

Table 6.6a ETFTable Select Sector SPDRs (As of October 5, 2009)

Printed with permission of www.etftable.com

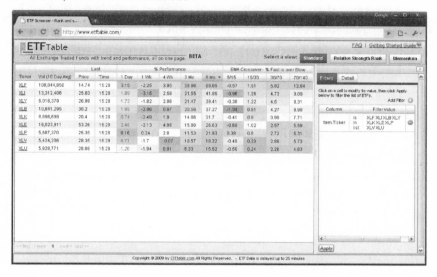

Table 6.6b ETFTable Relative Strength with Six-Month Ranking Selected (As of October 5, 2009)

Printed with permission of www.etftable.com

Composite Rankings on a Customized ETF List

Moreover, the Web site allows you to select your own set of ETFs for comparison by clicking the Filters tab to the right of the table. Click in the box under Column and highlight the word "ticker"; click the blank box next to that and highlight "is in list"; and then in the Filter Value column key in all the tickers separated by a space. (Remember, I provided these tickers in Appendix 6.1; just type them in with spaces or copy from the file you made in Word.) Lastly, click the Apply button. This action saves the list so that the next time you open the site on the same computer, it will automatically appear. This is the same process that I used to place the SPDR ETFs in a separate file in Table 6.6a and 6.6b.

Table 6.6c contains only page 1 of our entire universe of ETFs showing the six-month top performers. Likewise, Table 6.6d provides page 1 of the RS rankings for this same universe. To obtain these two tables, just follow the instructions in the preceding paragraph.

You can see by viewing these tables that the three best-performing ETFs were all international—IDX (Market Vectors Indonesia), TUR (iShares MSCI Turkey), and RSX (Market Vectors Russia). Even over the four shorter time frames (see Table 6.6d) of one day through three months, the TUR and RSX ETFs have extremely high relative strength rankings. But IDX has started to substantially weaken over the past week. This may indicate that IDX will soon drop from the top rankings, but as of October 12, 2009, it was still in the top rankings based on the six-month relative strength.

Table 6.6c ETFTable Selected ETF Universe (Data As of 10/12/2009; Only Page 1 Shown)

Printed with permission of www.etftable.com

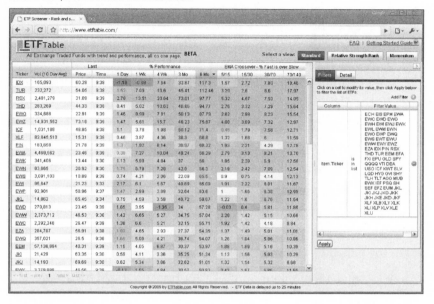

Table 6.6d ETFTable Relative Strength Rank of Selected Universe with Six-Month Ranking Selected (Data As of 10/12/2009; Only Page 1 Shown)

Printed with permission of www.etftable.com

Other ETF Web Sites with Performance Data

Another Web site, www.etftrends.com, ranks funds by performance (percent price change) using one-day, one-week, two-week, four-week, three-month, six-month, and one-year time frames. You can click on any column heading and array the data in ascending or descending order. However, no relative strength ranking is provided. Here is the URL:

www.etftrends.com/etf-tools/etf-analyzer/?sort=
PCCH26W&dir=ASC&pg=1&flt=

Another source of ETF performance data is *Investor's Business Daily*. The newspaper has a section on the top-ranked ETFs using their own proprietary ranking criteria. *SmartMoney* magazine has an ETF Tracker, but shows only performance for the past week. The URL for that site is this:

www.smartmoney.com/etf/etfTickerTracker/?tkrMode=wtd

An interesting site is www.ETFinvestmentoutlook.com. It tracks about 100 ETFs and analyzes ETFs with price and volume, as well as the McClellan oscillators. It shows the percentage of issues in each ETF that are declining or advancing. And you can quickly access a chart with useful information with a mouse click.

Appendix 6.1: Listing of ETF Symbols for Composite Performance and Ranking Tables

ECH EIS EEM EWA EWC EWD EWG EWH EWI EWJ EWK EWL EWM EWN EWO EWP EWQ EWS EWT EWU EWW EWY EWZ EZA IDX PIN RSX THD TUR EEM EFA FXI EPU GLD SPY QQQQ VTI DBA USO ICF KWT SLV LQD HYG GVI SHY TLH TLT AGG MUB BWX IEF PSQ SH SEF EFZ EUM JKL JKI JKJ JKG JKK JKH JKE JKD JKF XLF XLB XLY XLK XLI XLP XLV XLE XLU

Endnotes

1 Colby, Robert W. "Sticking with Strength: Applying the Relative Strength Strategy to ETFs." TradingEducation.com, May 25, 2006.

2 www.robertwcolby.com.

3 "Backtesting a Sector Momentum Strategy," October 18, 2009.

7

Subscription Software for Ranking the ETF Universe

"The investor's chief problem—and even his worst enemy—is likely to be himself."

Benjamin Graham (1894-1976), legendary American investor, scholar, teacher, and coauthor of the 1934 classic *Security Analysis*

"Let the market tell you where to invest your money."[1]

Sam Stovall, chief investment strategist for Standard & Poor's Equity Research Services

The number and capabilities of online investing software programs have greatly improved over the past few years. And their screening capability keeps improving all the time. I have written reviews of two specific software programs for *Technical Analysis of Stocks & Commodities*. Those two programs are covered in this chapter because they both can sort and analyze our entire ETF universe in a myriad of ways or in any number of portfolio subsets that the user cares to follow. A brief description of each software's ETF screening capability is provided in the text that follows. In actuality, both services contain a much broader array of other analytical features that can be used by traders and investors. The ETF screening capability is just one small sliver of these services' enormous power. Their software can also analyze thousands of individual stocks on a fundamental and technical basis, and each program offers a unique approach to accomplish their stated goals. I have also provided the related Web site addresses for those investors who would like a trial run of these software programs.

High Growth Stock Investor Software (HGSI)

High Growth Stock Investor is a service used by professional investors and traders. First you need to download the program to your computer's hard drive. Nightly updates provide the latest end-of-day data after your initial download. Since all the information is stored on your hard drive, you can view the program without being connected to the Internet. This is a great feature because you can be anywhere and access the program and do your market analysis when you have the time. However, to update the files you need to connect to the Internet, either hardwired or wireless.

This software program focuses on analyzing and ranking large groups of stocks and ETFs. This group-level analysis allows you to quickly organize or reorganize groups as a technique to narrow down the market to a small number of potentially high-growth-oriented stocks and ETFs. *Unique to HGSI is its capability to generate a variety of indexes for your custom-made groups. This feature then lets you compare the indexes from multiple groups to determine group relative strength.* Among the many other tools is an extremely flexible ranking system, a powerful filtering system, and advanced charting. You can search the database for stocks and ETFs that meet your specific requirements using a powerful set of search operators. These operators evaluate more than 400 data fields of information for each stock or index and quickly produce a list for further examination. Give the search a filter name to save it into the list of filters. Programming skill is not necessary.

HGSI software offers investors and traders a wealth of screening tools, filters, indicators, charts, and customizable features that provide a significant opportunity to uncover the cream of the crop among U.S. stocks (more than 9,000 at last count) and ETFs (the entire universe). For stocks, the site can analyze data on Earnings Growth, Relative Strength, and Group Strength that are highly ranked to get the best bang for the buck. The data can be analyzed as percentages or ranked from 99 to 1, on any time frame such as by weeks for any specific number of weeks—2, 4, 6, 8, 13, 26, and so on. The 26-week data translates into a six-month time frame, exactly our focus for determining ETF performance. Thus, you can observe the actual percentage change over that time frame in one table for all weeks going back in time, and also sort on an older week to see how the current ranking is impacted. The software applies the concept of Group Strength and Group Speed (momentum) to the data so that you can pinpoint when the market is rotating from one group to another. You can find which ETFs are increasing in strength as well as the rate of change or speed of the change, and thus focus on the strongest ones.

HGSI Capabilities

With the HGSI software, you can carry out these tasks:

1. Track movement in industries and sectors.
2. Be proactive in identifying and responding to trends in relevant markets, sectors, and industries.
3. See which ETFs are reaching new highs or lows. See the number of advancing or declining stocks in comparable market indexes.

4. Track real-time data for your portfolio or any custom group using the QuoteTracker integration.

5. Make buying or selling decisions based on up-to-the-minute data.

6. Find the best stocks, ETFs, or mutual funds for your investment strategy.

7. Search for stocks and ETFs using the easy-to-use filter language to create a list of potential candidates.

8. Analyze for chart patterns using candlesticks, moving-average crossovers, Wilder directional movement, and more. There are more than 50 charting indicators that can be selected.

9. Use premade SmartGroup searches, designed for various styles of investing such as dividend investing or growth investing or ETF investing. SmartGroups are filter-created groups that are updated each time you update the stock database.

10. Refine your search by ranking stocks according to the criteria you select. Choose from more than 400 technicals and fundamentals, such as Relative Strength Price-to-Sales Ratio (used by Charles Kirkpatrick in his work in conjunction with price relative strength), Up/Down Volume Ratio, Earnings Rank, or Revenue Rank.

11. Use filters developed by Charles Kirkpatrick to select stocks using three portfolios: value, bargain, and growth. The Value and Bargain were previously implemented in HGSI. Now the Kirkpatrick Chart Pattern warehouse column and filter for the Growth portfolio have been added.

ETF Coverage

Figure 7.1 provides a view of how ETFs are arrayed in different groups for analysis—by category, by bull or bear, and by family. And of course you can customize the scan you want to see and save it for future analysis.

Figure 7.1   ETF universe coverage

Edit Filter

Figure 7.2 shows a sample of an edit filter that is applied to the ProShares family of ETFs shown in Figure 7.1. This filter is selecting ETFs for particular setups.

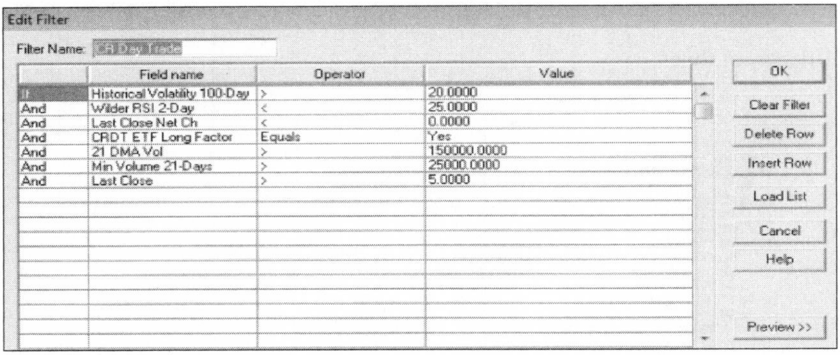

Figure 7.2   Edit filter example

ETF Relative Strength Ranking

After you have a list of ETFs that meet your requirements, you can use two very powerful tools to rank them. Using the interactive ranking tool, shown in Figure 7.3, you can rank all the ETFs in the group (in this screen the ProShares UltraShort funds were ranked) using various relative strength types, such as Wilder RSI, Percent Change, and Comparative RS to another security. A spreadsheet-like window displays color-coded historical relative strength, velocity, and acceleration for each ETF.

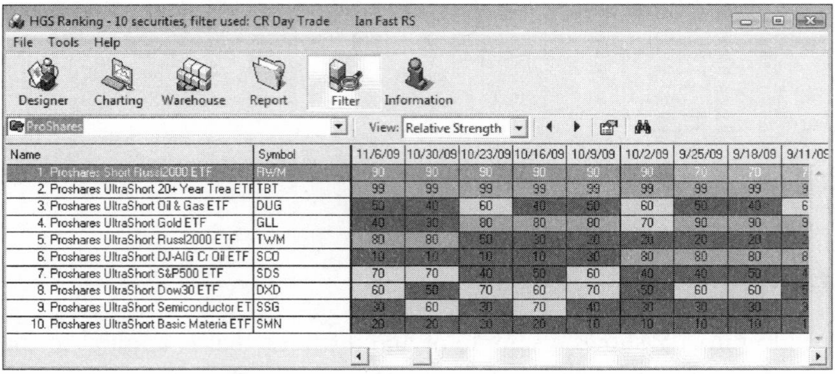

Figure 7.3   HGSI 26 week ranking module for ProShares UltraShort funds only

Figure 7.3 shows a 26-week relative strength ranking of the ProShares ETFs selected by the filter shown in Figure 7.2. As you can see, the Short Russell 2000 and UltraShort 20+ Year Treasury were on top of the list in this example. With the click of a mouse, you highlight an earlier week—for example, 10/23/09—and see the top ranking that week. All the other columns then adjust accordingly. This allows you to see how it performed from that point forward and backward in time which is quite a nice feature.

ETF 26-Week Price Performance

Figure 7.4 displays the same ten ETFs listed in Figure 7.3 but this time showing the actual percentage change for the same 26-week period. As you can see in the actual program, the change from red to yellow to green provides a quick visual image to the change in performance, and vice versa. With this type of analysis there is no need to listen to the Wall Street gurus' predictions of what is moving. With HGSI you can pay attention to what is actually moving and stay with the best performers for the strategy you are using.

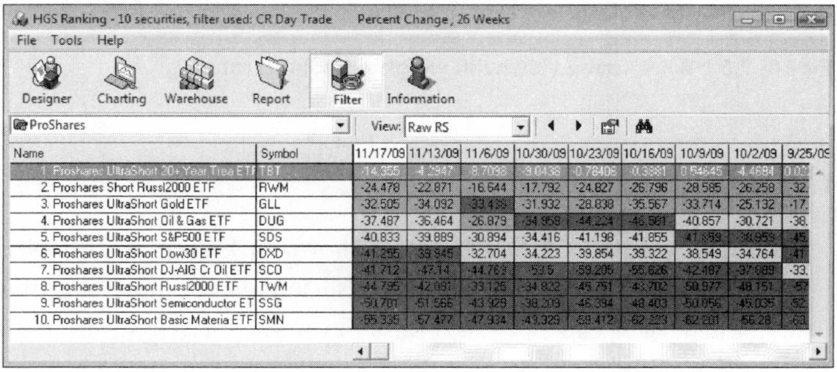

Figure 7.4   HGSI 26-week ranking module for actual percentage change for ProShares UltraShort funds

ETF Weighted Combination Ranking

Another approach to ranking ETFs is to use a weighted combination rank features within the Warehouse portion of the program, as shown in Figure 7.5. Using this method, you select as many data fields of information from the database as needed and assign weights (relative importance) to each data field. The ETFs in that group are then ranked on each of these fields, with the score combined to produce a final ranking. The end result is a weighted combination sort of all the ETFs in your group, bringing ETFs with the best combination to the top of the list. Figure 7.6 is ranking on historical volatility. You can use any of the hundreds of Warehouse data fields to create very complex rankings.

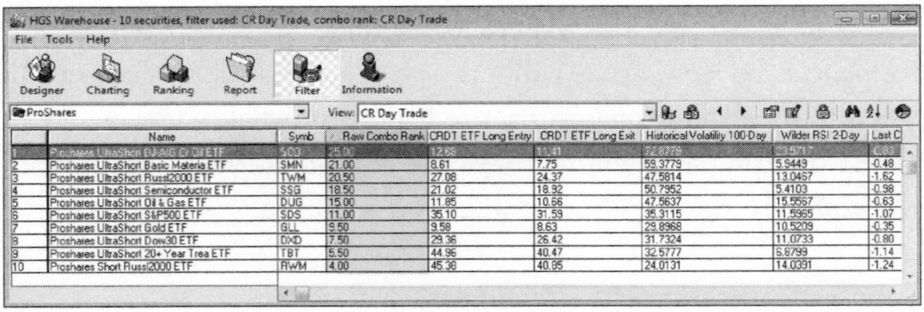

Figure 7.5   Warehouse view with weighted combo ranking

Charting Example and Indicators

The richly featured charting tool, shown in Figure 7.7, enables users to quickly analyze stocks and ETFs using one or more charting views. Each view can have several subwindows. Each subwindow can overlay multiple indicators or you can put different indicators into separate subwindows. An unlimited number of views can be created, each with different colors, indicators, annotations, and more. There are more than 50 indicators that cover a wide range of investment styles.

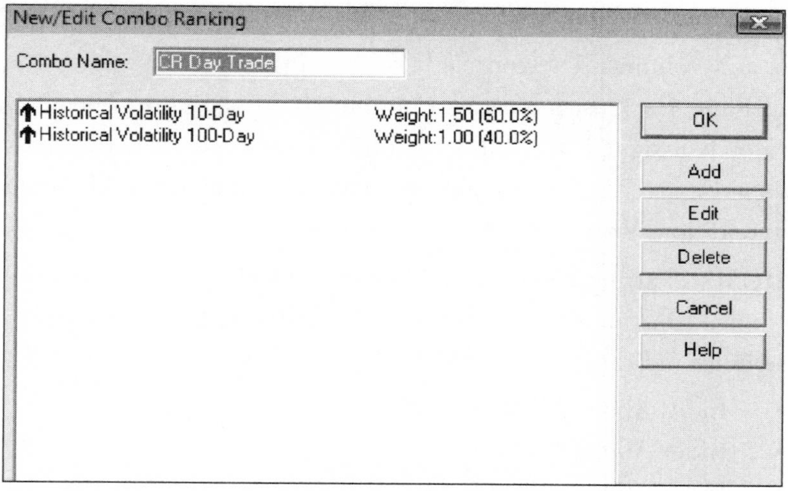

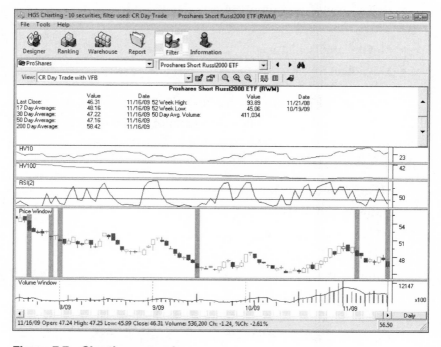

Figure 7.6   **Warehouse combo ranking rules**

Figure 7.7   **Charting example**

In Figure 7.7 there are five windows (HV10, HV100, RSI(2), Price, and Volume). The vertical bars are annotations applied by the Visual Filter Backtest indicator, a unique HGSI indicator. The VFB indicator is assigned to a filter (in this example we used the filter shown in Figure 7.2). The green vertical bars are telling you when the filter conditions were met.

HGSI's charting offers a number of "index"-specific indicators (not shown) that are not possible with standard charting applications. These index indicators include the following:

- % Index Above 20DMA
- % Index Above 30DMA
- % Index Above 50DMA
- Index % Accumulation/Distribution
- Index Adv/Dec Line
- Index Based Arms Indicator
- Index New High/Low Line
- McClellan Oscillator
- McClellan Summation Index

These types of indicators in traditional charting programs generally require importing the data in the form of a fake chart and other end-user manipulations. With HGSI the data is already computed with the index and can be directly charted.

HGSI Contact Information

Industry Monitors

HGSI

P. O. Box 760

Sumner, WA 98390

Phone: (253) 863-2389

E-mail Product Support: Support@highgrowthstock.com

For a free 60-day trial of the software and data, go to www. highgrowthstock.com/60daysfree.

Monthly subscription: $59

VectorVest Software

VectorVest U.S. is a powerful investing, back-testing, and port-folio management tool. A Real Time version is also offered, but that is not necessary for our purposes. VectorVest Online also offers versions for investors and traders in Canada, Australia, Europe, the United Kingdom, and South Africa.

After downloading the software, you can obtain the daily closing prices of all securities after hours by logging on to their Web site. One nice feature is that all the data resides on their computer and does not take up any space on your hard drive. Therefore, it takes only a few seconds to log in each night. Also, you can download data on to your laptop while you are traveling.

The program contains technical and fundamental data on more than 8,000 U.S. stocks, 190 industry groups, and 40 business sec-tors, as well as the entire U.S. ETF universe. There are a large num-ber of preset searches (strategies) for bull and bear markets to select stocks, as well as specific searches for the best ETFs that meet any criteria you select. Moreover, users can input their own search criteria and then back-test it for years with software plug-ins such as "AutoTester" (quick and easy back-testing on one strategy at a time) and the "Simulator" (detailed back-testing on many strate-gies simultaneously).

Market Timing Indicator

The software also provides a "Market Timing Indicator" (see Figure 7.8), which pinpoints market buy and sell signals based on combining the trends of its three proprietary indicators, the Price of the VectorVest Composite, the Relative Timing, and the Buy-to-Sell Ratio. VectorVest tracks the entire stock market using its own index called the VectorVest Composite. In addition there is a technical analysis add-on called ProTrader that charts any stock or ETF. (See

Figure 7.9.) Basic charts with moving averages of your choice are available for any ETF. The chart also includes a timing indicator to

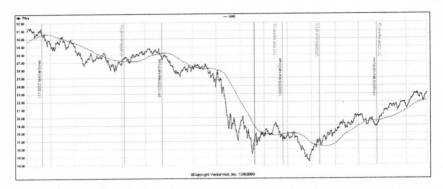

Figure 7.8   Market timing graph with confirmed buy and sell signals (October 2009)

Printed with permission of VectorVest

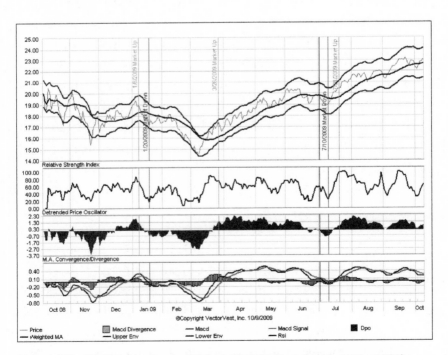

Figure 7.9   ProTrader chart with technical indicators (October 2009)

Printed with permission of VectorVest

show whether VectorVest considers an ETF to be a buy, sell, or hold. There is weekly video commentary available on Friday, and daily market updates on the best-performing searches for the day.

ETF Composite Price Performance Over 26 Weeks

Figure 7.10 illustrates the composite universe with six-month price performance for October 8, 2009. As you can see, the top three performers are Market Vectors Indonesia (113.97% return in six months), iShares MSCI Thailand (87.24%), and iShares MSCI Turkey (84.84%). Our ETF universe was input into a watch list and saved for future use and then also saved as a customized search. So all you need to do is open the program and go directly to the saved search to obtain the latest performance data.

VectorVest Contact Information

VectorVest, Inc.

20472 Chartwell Center Dr., Suite D

Cornelius, NC 28031

Product Support: (704) 895-4095; Sales: (888) 658-7638

E-mail Product Support: support@vectorvest.com

Sales: sales@vectorvest.com

For a $9.95 trial, go to www.vectorvest.com/masonsontrial.

Monthly subscription: $59

Yearly subscription: $645 for end-of-day product

Endnotes

1 Stovall, Sam. *The Seven Rules of Wall Street: Crash-Tested Investment Strategies That Beat the Market*. McGraw-Hill, 2009.

UniSearch Tool   Resize

File • Find • Graph • History • Details • Print • Layout • Quick Test • Add To Watchlist • Analysis • News • Help

Date: 10/8/2009 ▾   Run Search   Return: 25   ☑ Return All

Edit   Sorted by: 26 Week Price Delta Desc, VST DESC

{New Search}

Return ○ Stocks   ○ Industries   ○ Business Sectors

Selected Date	Parameter	Operator	Value
Date of Search	Stock Watchlist	=	Book List
Date of Search	Stock Price - (Split Adjusted)	26 Week D	Sorted Descending

My Searches

Company	Symbol	26 Week Price Delta	26 Weeks ago Price	Exch.	Price	$ Change	%PRC	Value	RV	RS	RT	VST	GRT	REC	Stop	EPS	EY	P/E	GPE	D
MktVctrsIndia	IDX	113.07%	20.64	N	61.28	-1.06	-1.54	61.28	1.00	1.00	1.45	1.20	0	B	54.79	0.00	0.00	999.99	0.00	
iShrsMSCIThailn	THD	87.24%	23.35	N	43.72	+0.10	+0.23	43.72	1.00	1.00	1.48	1.20	0	B	38.52	0.00	0.00	999.99	0.00	
iShrsMSCITurky	TUR	84.84%	28.83	N	53.29	+1.26	+2.42	53.29	1.00	1.00	1.60	1.27	0	B	47.17	0.00	0.00	999.99	0.00	
Market Vctrs Rus	RSX	70.49%	17.45	xA	29.75	+1.36	+4.79	29.75	1.00	1.00	1.72	1.33	0	B	25.35	0.00	0.00	999.99	0.00	
iShr MsAus	EWD	70.20%	13.22	A	22.50	+0.51	+2.32	22.50	1.00	1.00	1.63	1.28	0	B	19.79	0.00	0.00	999.99	0.00	
iShr MsAusy	EWA	62.83%	14.42	xA	23.48	+0.85	+3.76	23.48	1.00	1.00	1.61	1.27	0	B	20.50	0.00	0.00	999.99	0.00	
iShr MsBra	EWZ	60.38%	44.70	xA	71.69	+1.72	+2.46	71.69	1.00	1.00	1.54	1.23	0	B	62.42	0.00	0.00	999.99	0.00	
iShr MsBlg	EWK	59.42%	8.33	A	13.28	+0.19	+1.45	13.28	1.00	1.00	1.47	1.20	0	B	11.84	0.00	0.00	999.99	0.00	
PwrShrsIndiaPrt	PIN	55.68%	13.90	xA	21.64	+0.30	+1.41	21.64	1.00	1.00	1.35	1.15	0	B	19.44	0.00	0.00	999.99	0.00	
iShr MsNth	EWN	55.13%	13.26	A	20.57	+0.41	+2.03	20.57	1.00	1.00	1.47	1.20	0	B	18.33	0.00	0.00	999.99	0.00	
iShr MsSng	EWS	54.81%	6.97	A	10.79	+0.12	+1.12	10.79	1.00	1.00	1.24	1.10	0	B	9.97	0.00	0.00	999.99	0.00	
iShr MsIta	EWI	52.98%	13.57	A	20.76	+0.23	+1.12	20.76	1.00	1.00	1.44	1.19	0	B	18.63	0.00	0.00	999.99	0.00	
iShr MsESp	EWP	50.40%	33.63	xA	50.58	+0.47	+0.94	50.58	1.00	1.00	1.37	1.16	0	B	45.88	0.00	0.00	999.99	0.00	
iShr MsCan	EWC	44.64%	18.01	xA	26.05	+0.52	+2.04	26.05	1.00	1.00	1.32	1.13	0	B	23.65	0.00	0.00	999.99	0.00	
iShr Silver	SLV	43.96%	12.17	xA	17.52	+0.27	+1.57	17.52	1.00	1.00	1.44	1.19	0	B	15.06	0.00	0.00	999.99	0.00	
iShr MsSoAfr	EZA	43.59%	39.46	xA	56.66	+0.78	+1.40	56.66	1.00	1.00	1.36	1.15	0	B	51.13	0.00	0.00	999.99	0.00	
Evolution Petro	EPM	43.56%	2.25	A	3.23	+0.17	+5.56	1.05	0.39	1.00	1.42	1.01	0	H	2.88	-0.07	-2.17	-46.14	-0.18	
iShr MsFra	EWQ	43.55%	18.23	A	26.17	+0.42	+1.63	26.17	1.00	1.00	1.40	1.17	0	B	23.61	0.00	0.00	999.99	0.00	
iShr MsSwe	EWD	43.26%	16.02	xA	22.95	+0.21	+0.92	22.95	1.00	1.00	1.24	1.10	0	B	21.44	0.00	0.00	999.99	0.00	
iShr MsMex	EWW	43.03%	31.93	xA	45.67	+0.57	+1.26	45.67	1.00	1.00	1.35	1.15	0	B	41.54	0.00	0.00	999.99	0.00	
iShr MngSmVal	JKL	42.76%	45.16	N	64.47	+1.05	+1.66	64.47	1.00	1.00	1.49	1.21	0	B	58.80	0.00	0.00	999.99	0.00	
iShr MsEmrgMKT	EEM	42.47%	27.95	xA	39.82	+0.48	+1.22	39.82	1.00	1.00	1.41	1.17	0	B	36.17	0.00	0.00	999.99	0.00	
S & P Finl	XLF	42.14%	10.63	xA	15.11	+0.02	+0.13	15.11	1.00	1.00	1.44	1.19	0	B	13.79	0.00	0.00	999.99	0.00	
iShr MSSK	EWY	40.32%	32.69	xA	45.87	+0.70	+1.55	45.87	1.00	1.00	1.30	1.13	0	B	41.98	0.00	0.00	999.99	0.00	
iShr MSUK	EWU	40.27%	11.10	xA	15.57	+0.14	+0.91	15.57	1.00	1.00	1.31	1.13	0	B	14.48	0.00	0.00	999.99	0.00	
iShr MSMay	EWM	39.74%	7.60	xA	10.62	+0.17	+1.63	10.62	1.00	1.00	1.29	1.12	0	B	9.66	0.00	0.00	999.99	0.00	
iShrs MSCI Isrl	EIS	39.53%	36.01	N	50.25	+0.465	+0.93	50.25	1.00	1.00	1.41	1.17	0	B	46.14	0.00	0.00	999.99	0.00	
iShr CohenkSt	ICF	38.78%	34.48	xA	47.85	+0.93	+1.98	47.85	1.00	1.00	1.47	1.20	0	B	43.81	0.00	0.00	999.99	0.00	
iShr MsTaiwn	EWT	38.38%	8.91	xA	12.33	-0.15	-1.20	12.33	1.00	1.00	1.25	1.10	0	B	11.21	0.00	0.00	999.99	0.00	
iShr MsSwi	EWL	37.85%	15.72	xA	21.67	+0.18	+0.84	21.67	1.00	1.00	1.30	1.12	0	B	19.83	0.00	0.00	999.99	0.00	
iShr MngMdVal	JKI	37.59%	45.57	N	62.70	+0.82	+1.33	62.70	1.00	1.00	1.43	1.19	0	B	57.35	0.00	0.00	999.99	0.00	
iShr MSHK	EWH	37.58%	11.39	xA	15.67	+0.25	+1.62	15.67	1.00	1.00	1.20	1.08	0	B	14.51	0.00	0.00	999.99	0.00	
iShr MSGer	EWG	37.36%	16.38	xA	22.50	+0.35	+1.58	22.50	1.00	1.00	1.36	1.15	0	B	20.40	0.00	0.00	999.99	0.00	

Figure 7.10   ETF universe ranked by 26-week price performance

Printed with permission of VectorVest

8

Putting It All Together

"In this century or the next it's still 'Buy low, sell high.'"
Sir John Templeton, *World Monitor: The Christian Science Monitor Monthly*, 1993

"It's time to recognize that things have changed and they will continue to change for the next—yes, the next 10 years and maybe even the next 20."
William H. Gross, manager of Pimco Total Return Fund[1]

"Odds are you don't know what the odds are."
Gary Belsky and Thomas Gilovich, *Why Smart People Make Big Money Mistakes*

To take advantage of the proactive investing strategy presented in this book, let's encapsulate the key steps provided in previous chapters so that all the critical information you need is in one place. After reading the earlier chapters, you may be overwhelmed by all the material presented or concerned that it may be difficult for you to follow or to implement the strategy presented. Don't be concerned at all, because you can learn to follow the approach in this book rather easily, since all the steps are provided and all the information you need is provided by free Web sites or in publicly available publications or in your local library. Even if you do not have a personal computer, most libraries offer that capability for free. It won't be as convenient as working at home, but it is an option. If you currently don't own a personal computer, hopefully this book will excite you enough to buy one just for your investment tracking, since the prices have come down to less than $500.

This chapter provides a review of the key elements of the strategy and how to execute it going forward. It may take you a couple of hours to get everything rolling for the first time, after you begin to follow the steps. Also, initially it will take you time to review and start tracking your existing investments. After you set up the process outlined in the book, you will find that monitoring the markets weekly doesn't take more than 15 minutes on the weekend, or for those of you who are quick, it may take about 5 minutes to get the market direction, another 5 minutes to download the top-performing ETFs, and a few minutes to set up your buy or sell orders for Monday morning. Following are the key steps for applying the insights that you need to focus on to become a successful investor.

Step 1: Determine Your Risk Tolerance and Investor Profile

The first step is to understand your stock market risk and your maximum drawdown. Chapter 2, "Understanding the Concept of Risk," focused on those issues, and you should be able to classify yourself as a conservative, moderate, aggressive, or very aggressive investor. Keep in mind that you may have different investor profiles for your retirement and nonretirement accounts due to your age, income, funds available for investment, years to retirement, and other factors. One interesting current report on investor psychology and risk is provided by Kiplinger's Personal Finance at www.kiplinger.com/reports/investor-psychology.

Step 2: Examine Existing Portfolios for Possible Reallocation

The second step is to review all of your existing investment statements and place them on individual spreadsheets or in separate portfolios, using one of the many free financial Internet sites. Then you need to review the current asset allocations of each portfolio and determine whether you need to reallocate your holdings going forward. You want your portfolios to have the risk tolerance and profile that you have determined based on input from Chapter 2. Moreover, whenever possible, when you sell an existing portfolio position you should consider replacing it with an ETF. Of course, in some retirement plans at your workplace, you may not have any ETF options. In that case try to mimic the top-ranked ETFs such as large growth, international, and bonds.

Step 3: Evaluate the Stock Market's Condition

The next step is to find out whether you should be buying, selling, or holding your portfolio positions. That is where the "Stock Market Dashboard" comes into the investing equation. Here you assess the market's condition using a group of unrelated indicators, waiting for a consensus "buy" or "sell" (a +3 or –3, respectively) signal based on analyzing the eight indicators in the dashboard. If you are using the dashboard for the first time, you may find that there is no clear-cut buy or sell signal at the moment, but instead a neutral signal in the range of +2 to –2 may be shown. You may also find that the last buy or sell signal occurred weeks or months ago. In those cases, you should wait for the next buy or sell signal. After you have been using the strategy for a time, all the signals should be taken as soon as they occur. Only when using the strategy for the first time would you have to decide in between signals what to do, if anything.

If the dashboard signal is +3 or more, you should put existing cash to work in the top-ranked ETFs. Similarly, if the composite signal is –3 or worse, you should sell all existing equities. The *optimal time to get in or out of the market is when the dashboard* first *gives a buy or sell signal,* not days, weeks or months later when the existing trend has been in place and the market has already made a big move in either direction. You want the odds in your favor; therefore, you need to act promptly.

Interpreting Dashboard Signals

The key dashboard indicators, their critical levels, and the assigned values are provided in Table 8.1.

TABLE 8.1   Interpreting Eight Dashboard Signals

Indicator Name	Critical High/Low Levels	Assigned Value
1. Percentage of NYSE Stocks Above Their 50-Day Moving Average	Less than 25% then rises	+1
	Greater than 75% then falls	–1
2. NASDAQ Composite Stock Index Crosses 100-Day Moving Average	Index crosses MA from below	+1
	Index crosses MA from above	–1
3. NYSE New *Daily* Highs Minus New *Daily* Lows	–750 or more and recedes	+1
Weekly New Highs as % of Total Issues Traded	25%+ and then declines	–1
	No signal change for 6 months	0
4. NYSE Bullish Percentage	Less than 30% and turns higher	+1
	More than 70% and declines	–1
	No signal change for 6 months	0
5. NASDAQ Composite with MACD	MACD crossover to upside	+1
	MACD crossover to downside	–1

TABLE 8.1 Interpreting Eight Dashboard Signals (continued)

Indicator Name	Critical High/Low Levels	Assigned Value
6. AAII Weekly Investor Sentiment Survey Bullish Percentage	Less than 25% and turns higher	+1
	More than 50% and turns lower	−1
	No signal change for 6 months	0
7. Best-Six-Months Strategy with MACD	MACD crossover up near November on S&P Index	+1
November through April	MACD crossover down near May on S&P Index	−1
May through October	A Reversal of MACD Buy or Sell Signal	0
8. NASDAQ Summation Index MA Crossover with MACD Confirmation	Price pierces 5-day ema to upside + MACD crossover at or near same date	+1
	Price pierces 5-day ema to downside + MACD crossover at or near same date	−1

Three Approaches to Buying ETF Positions on a Consensus Buy Signal

When you receive a +3 reading on the dashboard *for the first time* (after a neutral or a prior sell signal), you should consider investing any available cash, using one of the three approaches presented here or a variation that you feel is appropriate:

1. Invest 100% of your cash funds immediately in the appropriate ETFs. This is the most aggressive option and it provides an opportunity for the greatest profits because you are entering the market early in the up cycle.

2. Invest 80% of your cash with a +3 reading, then 15% for each additional positive reading. This approach gets you in the market more slowly but involves less risk than the first choice.

3. Invest 25% of your cash with a +3 reading and an additional 20% for each additional positive reading, except that when +7

is reached, you invest the remaining 15% of your funds, as detailed here:

25% with a +3

20% with a +4

20% with a +5

20% with a +6

15% with a +7

This is a conservative approach, in which you spread your money out in order to wait for additional confirming positive signals. Also, you may not get to a +8 signal so that level should not be necessary to be reached to be fully invested. Because the dashboard may never reach levels of +7 or +8, you may want to have all you available funds invested at a reading of +5 or + 6 to become fully invested.

Sell All Equity Positions on a Dashboard Sell Signal

On the other hand, if a dashboard sell signal (–3) is given *for the first time* (after a prior neutral or buy signal), then you should sell all equity positions. This will result in having a 100% cash position that can be invested in cash equivalents (for example, Internet bank money market funds, money market mutual funds and savings accounts) until the next buy signal is given. When a sell signal is given, aggressive, knowledgeable, and risk-aware investors may want to buy a small position (5% to 10% of assets) in one of the ProShares inverse funds such as PSQ that rises when the NASDAQ 100 index falls. I would not recommend that you buy a leveraged inverse fund, since you need complete knowledge about its risks and quirky compounding. Shorting the market requires skill, nerves of steel, and the ability to cover your short position at the first sign of a rally. So in summary, you should not short the market until you have years of successful investing under your belt and you know exactly what you are getting into.

Working Through Dashboard Signals Near the March 9, 2009, Market Low

To actually get a feel for working with the dashboard, let's observe the eight market indicator readings near the market's low in 2009. (Appendix 8.1 provides the same type of review at the market's high on October 9, 2007.) Following is the reading of each of the market indicators in March 2009 based on viewing the specific charts online or using the chart examples provided in Chapter 5, "The Stock Market Dashboard—Key Stock Market Indicators to Gauge the Market's Direction":

1. **Percentage of NYSE Stocks Below Their 50-Day Moving Average**

   Looking at Figure 5.4, you can see that the reading of this percentage was at about 5% in early March, and then turned up sharply. Since it dropped below the 25% marker (extremely low reading) and turned up, it gets a +1 score.

2. **NASDAQ Composite Stock Index Crosses Above the 100-Day Moving Average**

   Looking at Figure 5.5, we can see that the index crossed the moving average to the upside in mid-March. That gets a +1 score, because it pierced the moving average line.

3. **NYSE Daily New Highs Minus Daily New Lows**

   Looking at Figure 5.6, we can see that the indicator breached –750 (our minimum measurement for a market low point) and then turned up in early March. That gets a +1 score.

4. **NYSE Bullish Percentage**

   Looking at Figure 5.7, we can see that the low reading in the beginning of March 2009 was 14%, and then the reading rapidly turned up. Since the 30% marker was penetrated to the downside and then hit 14% before turning up, it gets a score of +1.

5. MACD Indicator on the NASDAQ Composite Index

Looking at Figure 5.9, we can see that the MACD upward crossover occurred in early March, giving it a score of +1. You will note that even though we are not using the 50-dma as a measurement in our scoring system, this index pierced that moving average a few days after the MACD crossover. That additional crossover adds another confirming indicator that is not being tabulated in our system.

6. AAII Weekly Investor Sentiment Survey Bullish Percentage

Looking at Figure 5.8, we can see a reading of below 20% in March that turned up the next week. Therefore, since the reading was below the 25% marker and turned up the next week, it receives a score of +1.

7. Best-Six-Months Strategy with the MACD Indicator

Since March 2009 is within the best-six-months period of October through April, it would normally retain the +1 score obtained in October/November based on an MACD buy signal (see Figure 5.10). *However, shortly after its MACD buy signal in late October 2008, it gave an MACD sell signal in November 2008, thereby negating the buy signal.* Therefore it was given a "0" score in November will be in place until the next seasonal buy signal in October 2009.

8. NASDAQ Summation Index Moving Average Crossover with MACD Confirmation

Looking at Figure 5.11, we can see that the 5-dma crossed over the index to the upside a bit before mid-March, giving it a score of +1.

In Summary

In summary, by early to mid-March 2009, seven indicators had a score of +1, and one had a score of "0." Thus, a high score was reached rather quickly. That score not only put the odds of profitable investing heavily in your favor, but also, more important, signaled the low at a key turning point that provides maximum opportunity for profit. At other times, you may find that the score ranges from 0 to +2. In that situation you get ready to make a move, but you don't pull the trigger until at least +3 is reached. One investing approach that makes sense, mentioned previously, is to invest 70% of your available funds when the +3 reading is reached, and then subsequently add 10% as each of the next three indicators triggers a buy signal. Using this approach increases the probability of a successful outcome with a reduced drawdown.

Step 4: Invest in the Recommended Universe of ETFs

As covered in Chapter 4, "Exchange-Traded Funds—The Most Suitable Investment Vehicles," after you have observed a dashboard buy signal you should consider investing in the recommended universe of 66 ETFs. You will have not only a diversified portfolio, but also one that should provide significant profits. The number of ETFs to be purchased in each of the five categories was presented in that chapter together with the percent of your total dollars to be invested in each category. This information is replicated below for your convenience. Your risk tolerance and investor profile dictate your investor profile category, but you are free to make adjustments as you see fit:

Conservative Investor Allocation
Morningstar style—13% (of capital) (2 ETFs)

SPDR Sectors—13% (2 ETFs)

iShares Countries—13% (6 ETFs)

Fixed Income—53% (4 ETFs)

Specialty—8% (1 ETF)

Moderate Investor Allocation
Morningstar style—20% (3 ETFs)
SPDR Sectors—20% (3 ETFs)
iShares Countries—13% (4 ETFs)
Fixed Income—34% (3 ETFs)
Specialty—13% (2 ETFs)

Aggressive Investor Allocation
Morningstar style—20% (3 ETFs)
SPDR Sectors—20% (3 ETFs)
iShares Countries—20% (5 ETFs)
Fixed Income—20%(2 ETFs)
Specialty—20% (2 ETFs)

Very Aggressive Investor Allocation
Morningstar style—20% (3 ETFs)
SPDR Sectors—20% (3 ETFs)
iShares Countries—40% (6 ETFs)
Fixed Income—0%
Specialty—20% (3 ETFs)

The complete list of the 66 recommended ETFs, 5 inverse funds, and 3 benchmarks is shown here.

Morningstar Style Box	Ticker Symbol
Large-cap growth	JKE
Large-cap core	JKD
Large-cap value	JKF
Mid-cap growth	JKH
Mid-cap core	JKG
Mid-cap value	JKI
Small-cap growth	JKK
Small-cap core	JKJ
Small-cap value	JKL

Select Sector SPDRs	Ticker Symbol
Consumer discretionary	XLY
Consumer staples	XLP
Financial	XLF
Energy	XLE
Healthcare	XLV
Industrial	XLI
Materials	XLB
Technology	XLK
Utilities	XLU

International—country funds*	Ticker Symbol
Chile	ECH
Israel	EIS
Peru	EPU
Australia	EWA
Canada	EWC
Sweden	EWD
Germany	EWG
Hong Kong	EWH
Italy	EWI
Japan	EWJ
Belgium	EWK
Switzerland	EWL
Malaysia	EWM
Netherlands	EWN
Austria	EWO
Spain	EWP

*(iShares unless otherwise specified)

International—country funds°	Ticker Symbol (continued)
France	EWQ
Singapore	EWS
Taiwan	EWT
United Kingdom	EWU
Mexico	EWW
South Korea	EWY
Brazil	EWZ
South Africa	EZA
Market Vectors Indonesia	IDX
PowerShares India	PIN
Market Vectors Russia	RSX
Thailand	THD
Turkey Invest Market	TUR
Emerging Markets	EEM
MSCI EFA	EFA
FTSE-Xinhua China 25	FXI

°(iShares unless otherwise specified)

Fixed Income	Ticker Symbol
Barclays Aggregate Bond	AGG
Barclays Int'l Tsy Bond	BWX
Barclays Intermediate Gov't Credit	GVI
iShares iBoxx $ High Yield	HYG
iShares Barclay 7-10 year Treasury	IEF
iShares iBoxx $ Invest. Grade Corp. Bond	LQD
iShares S&P National Muni	MUB
iShares Barclay 1-3 year Treasury	SHY
iShares Barclay 10-20 year Treasury	TLH
iShares Barclay 20 year Treasury	TLT

Specialty Funds	Ticker Symbol
SPDR Gold Shares	GLD
iShares Silver Trust	SLV
U.S. Oil Fund	USO
PowerShares DB Agriculture	DBA
iShares Cohen & Steers Realty Majors Index	ICF
Major Vectors Solar Energy	KWT

Inverse Funds	Ticker Symbol
ProShares Short S&P 500	SH
ProShares Short NASDAQ 100	PSQ
ProShares Short Financials	SEF
ProShares Short MSCI EAFE	EFZ
ProShares Short MSCI Emerging Markets	EUM

Benchmarks	Ticker Symbol
SPDR S&P 500 Index	SPY
PowerShares NASDAQ 100	QQQQ
Vanguard Total Stock Market	VTI

Step 5: Select Top-Ranked ETFs Based on Relative Strength Analysis

Continuing with our example in Step 3 with the "buy" signal from the dashboard in mid-March 2009 that identified a market turning point, our next step is to go online and access www.etfscreen.com or www.etftable.com to find the top-ranking ETFs. (Refer to Chapter 6, "Using Relative Strength Analysis to Determine Where to Invest," which contains tables for each of these sites, since reproducing them here would be redundant.) Alternatively, if you decided to subscribe to High Growth Stock Investor software or VectorVest online, as presented in the preceding chapter, for those results, you can access them. You then select the strongest 15 ETFs from among the five major asset classes, based on the breakdown shown in Step 1. You should follow your investor profile and invest in the number of ETFs in their classification with the highest ranking.

If you are a more aggressive investor, you can follow the same approach or you could consider looking at the entire 66-ETF universe as one composite and selecting the top 15 ETFs, irrespective of risk tolerance or classification. This approach is much more risky, but can provide you with substantially higher returns during a powerful stock market advance. Be aware that at certain times the international ETFs may dominate the top positions in the composite table, and you may not want to put all your eggs in the international basket. So if you want to invest in the top-ranked ETFs from the universe, be very careful and definitely use stop-loss orders and trailing stops, as the prices rise. This approach just discussed may be suitable for very aggressive investors who have discipline and investing experience. It is not recommended for investors with a normal risk tolerance range.

When to Sell ETFs That Fall in the Ranking

After you have your 15-ETF portfolio, each week you should monitor their latest week's *six-month ranking performance* to determine whether any ETF has dropped below half of its ETF ranking position. At that point that ETF should be sold and the highest-ranked non-duplicated ETF purchased with the proceeds of the sale to replace it. Thus, if an ETF drops to the following ranking positions in its category, it should be sold:

- 5th-ranked position or lower for the Morningstar style (9 ETFs)
- 5th-ranked position or lower for the SPDR sectors (9 ETFs)
- 6th-ranked position or lower for the fixed income (10 ETFs)
- 17th-ranked position or lower for the international ETFs (32 ETFs)
- 4th-ranked position or lower for specialty ETFs (6 ETFs)

Step 6: Protect Your Portfolio Using Stops

Even with our careful and methodical investing approach, you need to understand that profits are not guaranteed. Therefore, after you make every ETF purchase, you should always consider placing a stop-loss order immediately. Moreover, also consider using trailing stops after a position starts making money. Alternatively, instead of using stops, you could buy put options on the major indices or buy an inverse ETF. However, those choices are more costly and will decay rapidly in price, if the market continues to rise.

Refrain from Refining Your Investing Plan

After you have begun using the investing methodology outlined in this book, you may want to refine it because it may not be working perfectly—that would be a big mistake. Do not make any changes or take on added risk, or invest too aggressively if you are a conservative person, or neglect to place stops. If you do any of these things, you may find that you are losing money and not enjoying yourself. Buy and sell rules are made to be followed 100% of the time or you'll find that they have no value at all. Do not decide to take a few of the buy and sell signals and not others. That approach can lead to a financial disaster.

Remember that taking profits is the name of the game in investing. And remember not to let taxes be a major determinant of when to sell. And, above all, don't let your emotions overrule your investing plan; otherwise, you will continually make the same mistakes. You need to work with the investing plan in up and down markets to become comfortable with it. There may be a few whipsaws along the way in which the dashboard buy and sell signals occur within a month of each other. That is always possible, but it should not be of concern because you will end up on the correct side of the market for its move higher.

Four Interesting Insights to Ponder

During the financial crisis, investors were in a tizzy not knowing what to do with their investments. Most investors held their positions mostly because they were scared. I remember reading an investor survey undertaken during the latest financial crisis. The survey found that the typical investor lost 35% of his or her market value in the decline, but about a quarter lost almost 50%. Moreover, the survey found that investors experienced varying emotions during this difficult period. The most common emotions reported by most of the respondents were being somewhat furious, apprehensive, and gloomy. More than 50% said it was probably a good buying opportunity, but they couldn't pull the trigger. Based on this survey, you should realize that being a successful investor requires that you minimize your emotional reaction to the markets and use a systematic, logical, and defensive approach. Otherwise your future results may not be what you expect.

A number of investment advisors are now reporting that more and more of their clients are becoming too aggressive now after the S&P 500 is up more than 56% from its March lows, and want to put their cash to work by buying equities. These investors want to get back to even, and they are not focusing on the risk, but rather on making money.[2] That's how investors act at market tops—they can't wait to get back in. Greed takes over their emotions, causing them to make bad decisions. That is why using the approach delineated in this book will help you make realistic, logical decisions.

It appears that, after the latest bear market beating, increased numbers of financial advisors are questioning the validity of a buy-and-hold approach. According to a September survey of financial advisors, 12.5% of respondents did not now believe in buy-and-hold investing, and 49.6% indicated that they would be quicker to make major portfolio changes under certain conditions.[3] If these advisors are finally waking up to the shortfalls of buy-and-hold, then it is certainly time for investors to also question its validity in light of their own investment experience.

A Bankrate survey of workers produced the following results when asked about how the financial crisis will impact their retirement plans:[4]

Response	Percentage
Retire on time	31%
One to five years later than planned	20%
Six to ten years later than planned	13%
More than 10 years later than planned	7%
Never able to retire	18%
Don't know or didn't answer	11%

Thus, the survey indicated that 58% of workers believe they will have some sort of delay in their retirement plans, whereas 25% expect to wait more than ten years or never retire. One way for you to avoid delaying your retirement is to be a smart proactive investor. That's now possible because you have an investing plan to work with and you know how to execute it to meet your financial goals.

A Last Word

Now that you have completed this instructive journey, learning about a nonemotional indicator-based approach to investing, I hope that you have benefited from your experience. If you have any questions or comments, please contact me at **les@buydonthold.com**, and I'll respond accordingly. I've also set up a Web site for further information on the strategy presented in this book at **www.buydonthold.com**. Visit the Web site for updates and other useful insights on investing. I wish you much success and hope that you join me on the road to stock market profits for many years to come.

Appendix 8.1: October 2007 Dashboard Scores

At the end of Step 3, I provided the specific dashboard readings near the March 2009 lows so that you could see firsthand how to use and interpret the signals. Likewise, to provide you with similar insight near a market top, I've selected the last top in October 2007 to again illustrate the dashboard's usefulness and timeliness. To get the most out of this review, refer to the charts from Chapter 5 or instead bring them up on your computer. Note that if you are using the free version of stockcharts.com for specific charts, remember that the charts only go back three years so, depending upon when you pull up the charts, the data for 2007 may not be available. Earlier data requires a subscription, as mentioned in that chapter.

Now, let's go through the dashboard signals near the market high on October 9, 2007:

1. **Percentage of NYSE Stocks Above Their 50-Day Moving Average**

   Looking back at Figure 5.4, you can see a percentage peak at about 80% twice in October 2007 and then a turn down. Since it dropped below the 75% marker and then turned down, it gets a –1 score.

2. **NASDAQ Composite Stock Index Crosses Below the 100-Day Moving Average**

   Looking at Figure 5.5, we can see that the index crossed the moving average to the downside in *mid-September 2007*. That gets a +1 score because it pierced the moving average line to the downside.

3. **NYSE Daily New Highs Minus Daily New Lows**

   We need to look at the number of new weekly highs as a percentage of all issues traded that week, since this indicator does not provide a useful market-high reading. So we need to go to

Barron's paper or online edition (Market Laboratory section). You can access this information weekly with the online or newspaper subscription or go to your local library to view the issue. This indicator did have a reading of 25%+ in July 2007, so it is given a score of +1.

4. NYSE Bullish Percentage

Looking at Figure 5.7, we can see the high point in early July 2007 at 74% and then the turn downward. *This gets a score of –1 in July 2007,* because it breached our 70% extreme point and headed downward way ahead of the market top in October. This signal was three months early but a clear warning that the underlying market was potentially decaying. By early October the reading of this indicator was in the low 60s, well below the indicator's peak in July. So *this indicator was able to detect the changing market strength three months early!*

5. MACD Indicator on the NASDAQ Composite Index

Note that Figure 5.9 was not referenced for this indicator because it does not go back to October 2007 as Figure 5.5 does. Looking at Figure 5.5, we can see that the MACD moving average crossover down signal occurred in mid-October 2007, thus getting a score of –1. You will also note that even though we are not using the 200-dma (shown on the chart in the figure) as a measurement in our scoring system, this index pierced that moving average to the downside in the beginning of January 2008.

6. AAII Weekly Investor Sentiment Survey Bullish Percentage

Looking at Figure 5.8, we can see a reading of about 54% that turned down the next week. Therefore, since the reading was above 50% and turned down, it receives a score of –1.

7. **Best-Six-Months Strategy with the MACD Indicator**

Looking at Figure 5.10, we find that the MACD had a *negative crossover* in mid-October 2007 instead of a seasonally expected positive crossover with a score of +1. So this indicator is rated a "0" going forward for the entire favorable period.

8. **NASDAQ Summation Index Moving Average Crossover with MACD Confirmation**

You need to go to www.stockcharts.com and put up a chart for $NASI with a 5-ema to see the data back to 2007 since Figure 5.11 only went back to September 2008. When you find the chart you will see that the index crossed over the 5-dma to the downside at the end of October 2007, giving it a score of –1.

In Summary

By mid-October 2007, *five* indicators had a score of –1, and two indicators were positive, and one indicator was neutral. In total, the dashboard score was –3. Thus this market top was identified very well, and it provided an opportunity to get out of the market with your portfolio intact from the ensuing collapse. This turned out to be a great exit point because the market cascaded downward over 50% with intermittent rallies until the low of March 9, 2009, when the dashboard correctly identified the bottom, as shown in our earlier example.

Endnotes

1 Farzad, Roben. "Searching for True North." *BusinessWeek*, October 5, 2009.

2 Jamieson, Dan. "Good or bad, greed is back." *InvestmentNews*, September 28, 2009.

3 Benjamin, Jeff. "In the active-passive debate, a fusion yields best results." *InvestmentNews*, November 16, 2009, p. 55.

4 Ruffenach, Glenn. "Have You Learned Your Lessons Yet." *The Wall Street Journal*, November 14, 2009, p. R4.

Bibliography

Appel, Gerald. *Opportunity Investing: How to Profit When Stocks Advance, Stocks Decline, Inflation Runs Rampant, Prices Fall, Oil Prices Hit the Roof,...and Every Time in Between*. FT Press, 2006.

Appel, Marvin. *Investing with Exchange-Traded Funds Made Easy: A Start-to-Finish Plan to Reduce Costs and Achieve Higher Returns*, Second Edition. FT Press, 2008.

Carr, Michael J. *Smarter Investing in Any Economy: The Definitive Guide to Relative Strength Investing*. W-A Publishing, 2008.

Colby, Robert W. *The Encyclopedia of Technical Market Indicators*, Second Edition. McGraw-Hill, 2003.

Covel, Michael. *Trend Following: Learn to Make Millions in Up or Down Markets*. FT Press, 2009.

Davis, Ned. *Being Right or Making Money*. Ned Davis Research, 2000.

El-Erian, Mohamed. *When Markets Collide: Investment Strategies for the Age of Global Economic Change*. McGraw-Hill, 2008.

Faber, Mebane T., and Richardson, Eric W. *The Ivy Portfolio: How to Invest Like the Top Endowments and Avoid Bear Markets*. John Wiley & Sons, Inc., 2009.

Frankle, Neal. *Why Smart People Lose a Fortune*. Just Write, 2004.

Gladwell, Malcolm. *Outliers: The Story of Success*. Little, Brown and Company, 2008.

Hayden, Vern; Webber, Maura; and Heller, Jamie. *Getting an Investing Game Plan: Creating It, Working It, Winning It*. John Wiley & Sons, Inc., 2003.

Hayes, Timothy. *The Research Driven Investor: How to Use Information, Data and Analysis for Investment Success*. McGraw-Hill Companies, 2000.

Headley, Price. *Big Trends in Trading: Strategies to Master Major Market Moves*. John Wiley & Sons, Inc., 2002.

Hirsch, Jeffrey A. and Hirsch, Yale. *Stock Trader's Almanac 2010*. John Wiley & Sons, Inc., 2010.

Kaeppel, Jay. *Seasonal Stock Market Trends: The Definitive Guide to Calendar-Based Stock Market Trading*. John Wiley & Sons, Inc., 2009.

Kirkpatrick, Charles D. *Beat the Market: Invest by Knowing What Stocks to Buy and What Stocks to Sell*. FT Press, 2008.

Kirkpatrick, Charles D., and Dahlquist, Julie R. *Technical Analysis: The Complete Resource for Financial Market Technicians*. FT Press, 2006.

LeFevre, Edwin, and Markman, Jon D. *Reminiscences of a Stock Operator*. John Wiley & Sons, Inc., 2009.

Levy, Robert. *The Relative Strength Concept of Common Stock Price Forecasting*. Investors Intelligence, 1968.

Lydon, Tom. *The ETF Trend Following Playbook: Profiting from Trends in Bull or Bear Markets with Exchanged Traded Funds*. FT Press, 2009.

Merriman, Paul. *Live It Up without Outliving Your Money! 10 Steps to a Perfect Retirement Portfolio*. John Wiley & Sons, Inc., 2008.

Morris, Gregory. *Candlestick Charting Explained: Timeless Techniques for Trading Stocks and Futures*. McGraw-Hill, 2006.

Murphy, John. *Technical Analysis of the Financial Markets: A Comprehensive Guide to Trading Methods and Applications*. Prentice Hall Press, 1999.

O'Neil, William. *How to Make Money in Stocks: A Winning System in Good Times or Bad*, Fourth Edition. McGraw-Hill, 2009.

Schwager, Jack D. *Market Wizards: Interviews with Top Traders*. HarperCollins, 1993.

Siegel, Jeremy. *Stocks for the Long Run: The Definitive Guide to Financial Market Returns & Long Term Investment Strategies*, Fourth Edition. McGraw-Hill, 2007.

Steenbarger, Brett N. *The Psychology of Trading: Tools and Techniques for Minding the Markets*. John Wiley & Sons, Inc., 2002.

Stovall, Sam. *The Seven Rules of Wall Street: Crash-Tested Investment Strategies That Beat the Market*. McGraw-Hill, 2009.

Taleb, Nassim Nicholas. *The Black Swan: The Impact of the Highly Improbable*. Random House, 2007.

Taleb, Nassim Nicholas. *Fooled by Randomness: The Hidden Role of Chance in Life and Markets*. Random House, 2008.

Weinstein, Stan. *Stan Weinstein's Secrets for Profiting in Bull and Bear Markets*. McGraw-Hill, 1988.

Wild, Russell. *Exchange-Traded Funds For Dummies*. Wiley, 2006.

Williams, Larry R. *The Right Stock at the Right Time: Prospering in the Coming Good Years*. John Wiley & Sons, Inc., 2003.

Zweig, Martin. *Martin Zweig's Winning on Wall Street*. Warner Books Grand Central Publishing, 1997.

INDEX

Numbers

26-week price performance
  HGSI, 179
  VectorVest software, 186
401(k)s, 58. *See also* retirement
403(b)s, 58. *See also* retirement

A

AAII (American Association of
  Individual Investors), 105
  Weekly Investor Sentiment Survey
    Bullish Percentage, 105, 114, 128,
    194, 205
accounts, retirement, 62-66
active mutual fund investing
  recommendations, 68, 70-71
AIG, 98
allocations
  of ETFs, 86-87
  stocks vs. bonds, 57
American Association of Individual
  Investors. *See* AAII
Ameriprise Financial Inc., 86
analysis, relative strength analysis
  (RSA), 60-61
  basics, 135-140
  ETFs, 141-144
  ranking ETFs, 145-154, 157-166, 170
annual management fees, 72
arguments for and against
  buy-and-hold (BAH), 21-24
Assessment Service, 41

assets
  classes, 17
  leveraging, 28
assets under management (AUM), 24
average true range (ATR), 51

B

Bankrate survey, 203
bankruptcy, 28
Barclays Wealth, 41
Barron's, 58, 111
bear markets
  duration of, 18
  impact on retirement plans, 62
  influences on, 27-31
  losses, 21, 29
  recoveries, 16
  secular, 14, 30
Bear Stearns, 28, 98
benefits of ETFs, 83
Best-Six-Months Strategy with
  MACD Indicator, 106, 117-121,
  130, 194, 206
bid-ask spreads, costs of, 25
BlackRock's iShares, 88
Bogle, John, 70
bonds
  ETFs, 59-61. *See also* ETFs
    (exchange-traded funds)
  long-term, 17
  market condition, reviewing, 58-59
  portfolio turnover rates, 25

FINANCIAL TIMES

In an increasingly competitive world, it is quality
of thinking that gives an edge—an idea that opens new
doors, a technique that solves a problem, or an insight
that simply helps make sense of it all.

We work with leading authors in the various arenas
of business and finance to bring cutting-edge thinking
and best-learning practices to a global market.

It is our goal to create world-class print publications
and electronic products that give readers
knowledge and understanding that can then be
applied, whether studying or at work.

To find out more about our business
products, you can visit us at www.ftpress.com.